ECONOMICS

IN THE NEWS

Based on Articles from The Economist

Brian Atkinson

University of Central Lancashire

ADDISON-WESLEY PUBLISHING COMPANY

WOKINGHAM, ENGLAND • READING, MASSACHUSETTS • MENLO PARK, CALIFORNIA
NEW YORK • DON MILLS, ONTARIO • AMSTERDAM • BONN • SYDNEY
SINGAPORE • TOKYO • MADRID • SAN JUAN • MILAN
MEXICO CITY • PARIS • SEOUL • TAIPEI

All articles are presented in the editorial style of the source newspaper.

Text design and typesetting by Express Graphics Ltd
Cover designed by Viva Design Ltd, Oxford
Printed by T. J. Press, Padstow, Cornwall

The cartoon has been reproduced with
permission from *NEA Inc.*

Contents

PART G: Comparative Economics   58

PART H: People and Methods   67

Introduction

A knowledge of economics helps us understand the world we live in and gives us the ability to realize when politicians and others are talking economic nonsense. Although facts and theories lie at the heart of the subject, John Maynard Keynes, one of this century's most influential economists, described economics as a method of thinking. This book aims to help you develop the way you think about economics and your mastery of the subject by encouraging you to apply economic theories and concepts to the real world as seen through the eyes of The Economist.

Launched in 1843 to advocate the cause of free trade, The Economist is now one of the world's most authoritative and influential magazines. It is held in especially high regard for its coverage of economics and it prides itself on its reverence for facts and figures, integrity, consistency of principle, rational analysis and absolute clarity. On the other hand it is criticized by some for arrogance, absence of doubt and too-clever-by-halfery. Articles in the magazine are unsigned. They express the view of The Economist rather than individuals. That view includes a firm belief in the free market and a hatred of capital punishment, the erosion of civil liberties and discrimination of any kind.

Some of the 38 extracts are abridged versions of longer articles. Otherwise they appear as when originally published. All other material such as the analysis of points made in the articles is, of course, my own. The articles have been chosen to illustrate a broad range of subject matter. Reading them will increase your understanding of economics even if you do not answer the questions included at the end of each (most) of the extracts.

The material can be used in a number of ways – for self-study, as a basis for seminar discussion, or for assessment. Similarly, the data can be analysed in different ways, and two of these are illustrated in the book. One approach is to summarize the material and then analyse it. Elsewhere, actual student answers are commented on to highlight common problems. My thanks go to Neil Greenwood, Charles Mumford and Richard Cowan for allowing me to use their answers as examples.

Here are some hints to help you when reading articles on economics. First, ask yourself which concepts and theories are relevant. For example, an article about drugs might seem to have very little to do with economics, but core concepts such as supply and demand allow economists to analyse the underlying positon as the first reading shows.

Second, try to analyse the values of the author. Social scientists often ask 'Who says so?' It is not difficult to guess that politicians will be selective in the facts that they present and the arguments put forward. But you should remember that economists also have values, and that these will influence the arguments that they present. This is as true of The Economist as it is of anyone else. You should feel free to disagree with what is written in the articles.

Third, question what you read. Is the argument in the article really supported by the evidence? And is the evidence strong or weak? Is there any evidence in the article or elsewhere that could support an opposing point of view?

Good economics can lead to improved decision making, not only by politicians and business leaders, but also in our own lives. It is my hope that these articles will be both interesting in themselves and help you realize that economic factors underlie much of everyday life.

Enjoy your economics.

Brian Atkinson
University of Central Lancashire

PART A: DEMAND, SUPPLY, MARKETS, SUBSIDIES

The Success of Ecstasy

WHERE is the best place in Britain to get a sound education in classical economics? Try your local rave club, where recent developments on the 'ecstasy scene' are proving the near-universal applicability of market theory.

What do strobe lights, late nights, old-age pensioners, Dutch factories and consumer-protection groups have in common? Adam Smith knew. Ecstasy, known to the pharmacologically minded as methylene-dioxyamphetamine, or MDMA for short, is the favoured drug of the dance-club set, prized for its energising and inhibition dropping properties. It has enjoyed a steady increase in popularity since the late 1980s, and seems now to have reached equilibrium in both user numbers (500,000) and street price – about £18 per dose. The ecstasy business had a watershed year in 1990. To cut costs, Britain's marketers largely abandoned their home labs and struck deals with foreign suppliers, most of them in Holland. Manufacturers there could use existing labs to lower manufacturing costs. The move to offshore supply boosted margins and output, but at the expense of quality.

Cheaper drugs like MDA and MDEA are now sold as ecstasy, often cut with amphetamines or in hugely larger doses to mimic ecstasy's sudden energy boost. On the street, these drugs have become known as 'speedy ecstasy', or 'smacky E' and were the bane of the purist's recreational hours. Less psychoactive than their cousin drug, they are up to 50 times more toxic and ten times more concentrated.

With more than 1m young Britons attending raves each week – enough to drain profits away from pubs, as the Henley Centre, an economic consultancy, reported last month – a culture centred around the ravers' music, drugs and lifestyle has become firmly established. Information about ecstasy is shared in the form of comic books put out by consumer-awareness groups. The consumption of downers like temazepam (conveniently available in every gran's medicine cabinet) has skyrocketed to combat the effects of the less pure forms of ecstasy.

With sales of more than £700m per year in Britain, ecstasy in all its forms is one of the most popular consumer products in the country, at least among the 18–24-year-olds that regularly go to raves. However, it may yet prove to be a victim of its own success. Some ravers, introduced to amphetamines through bogus ecstasy, have found it suits them better than the 'quality' drug. Sales of amphetamines, priced below £5 per dose and available everywhere, are now growing far faster than sales of ecstasy.

What lies ahead in the ecstasy market? Some production is already moving farther afield to even cheaper labs in Hungary and Latvia. Investments in research and development are producing a veritable cornucopia of new products. There are 184 known derivatives of ecstasy's parent drug, many of which are thought to have psychoactive properties. Clubs in southern California have heard rumours of the coming of MDMNA, a more mood-altering form of ecstasy without apparent side-effects which can last up to 24 hours per dose.

Oh, by the way, ecstasy is illegal in Britain.

The Essence of the Story

- Adam Smith's classical ideas about markets can be applied to 'the ecstasy scene'.

- MDMA is prized for its inhibition-dropping qualities.

- The market of the drug is in equilibrium with 500,000 users and a price of £18 a dose.

- To cut costs, manufacturers moved abroad, but quality suffered as a result.

- Cheaper drugs, often cut with amphetamines, are now sold as ecstasy.

- Sales now exceed £700 million a year, and R&D is leading to new products.

- A culture centred around drugs and music has become established and drains profits from pubs.

- Ecstasy is illegal.

Background and Analysis

The article uses traditional economic analysis – demand, supply and equilibrium – to analyse a non-traditional market far removed from Adam Smith's world. The implication of this is that economic analysis is a powerful tool that can be applied to a wide range of circumstances.

The movement away from UK production has lowered costs and shifted the supply curve from S_0 to S_1 as shown in Fig.1.1.

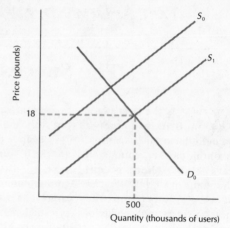

Figure 1.1

Research and development is providing competitive products. Economic theory suggests that this will lead to a fall in price. The analysis suggests that ecstasy and alcohol are competitive products. The success of ecstasy has reduced the demand for the services of pubs from D_0 to D_1 as shown in Fig. 1.2.

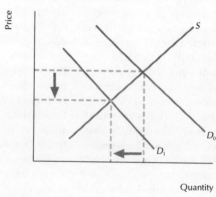

Figure 1.2

Why a Queue?

A queue, or a black market, is a sure sign that something – a ticket for Wimbledon, a dollar bill in Moscow is seriously underpriced. Or is it?

ANYWHERE in the world where young Italians gather, you will find a black market in Swatch watches. Buy one of the most sought-after models, the Chrono, the Scuba or the Automatic, for around £45, and you will have no trouble selling it again for twice as much. Take the watch to Italy, and it might fetch £300. Unsurprisingly, such Swatches are hard to come by. When stocks arrive they sell fast. Jewellers in London's Oxford Street, for instance, limit sales of these models to one a customer. Some expect punters also to buy a second, less fashionable, model as part of the deal.

The people at Swatch know all about this black market; indeed, some observers think they encourage it. Each Swatch model is sold at a fixed price throughout the world. The price is deliberately low – and supply is restricted. Only a few of each popular model will go to any particular shop, or area, at a time. Production of these models tends to be limited, sometimes to as few as 150, but more typically to between 5,000 and 15,000.

This is puzzling: queues and black markets are usually signs of under-pricing. Swatch, it seems, could make more money either by raising its prices or by expanding supply. What reason might there be for a producer to let queues form? How could that possibly maximise the company's expected profits?

Gary Becker, of the University of Chicago, chewed this over while dining out. Why, he pondered, did one restaurant refuse reservations and have a queue outside at peak times, when a similar one across the street seemed never more than half-full? Why did the restaurant with the queue not charge more? Being a fine economist, Mr Becker decided not to ask, but to work it out from first principles[1]. The answer, he argues, is that certain goods are demanded partly, if not primarily, because other people demand them, too. These are not 'Giffen goods' (where the relationship between demand and price is peculiar because the good makes up a large part of the consumer's budget).

Mr Becker is concerned with otherwise ordinary goods, that are preferred for their popularity. A queue is an indicator of this crowd effect. People want to eat at restaurants that are 'in', go to the 'big' game, see the new block-busting movie, pretend to have read the latest best-selling novel. It need not be that the queue is a mark of quality: as far as Mr Becker is concerned, what is in or out may be entirely arbitrary. But once something has been designated as 'in', people want it for that reason alone.

Perhaps this seems obvious. But next Mr Becker draws the demand curve for such a product, and suggests some striking properties. To begin with, Mr Becker surmises, the demand curve might slope downwards in the normal way: the cheaper the good, the greater the demand. But after a certain point, the good's popularity itself generates further demand, allowing the producer to raise the price and still sell more – that is, the demand curve slopes upwards. But eventually another turning-point is reached, where price rises begin to outweigh the good's popularity. Beyond this point, to achieve further increases in sales, prices must be cut again: in this third phase, the demand curve slopes downwards once more.

This means that there may be pairs of profit-maximising equilibriums for each producer of crowd-effect goods: a 'bad' equilibrium with unused capacity, and a 'good' one with queues. The question is, if you are in a bad one, what do you need to push you to a good one?

Plausible answers might be a willingness to gamble on enough promotional spending to start a bandwagon, and luck. In theory, as in life, you would expect bad equilibriums to be extremely common, and good ones extremely rare. Consider what happens when a restaurant in a good equilibrium raises its prices to trim its queues a little: at a price just pennies higher than £20, demand crashes back to almost nothing. A good equilibrium is highly unstable. The £20 price had been supported by a bubble of popularity, which then popped, sending demand down to its 'real' level. This could explain why producers of 'in' goods often choose not to increase supply: investing in extra capacity is risky. For a firm in a bad equilibrium, a small change in price causes only a small change in demand – the normal case. In a bad equilibrium, at least you are secure. Owners of fashionable restaurants with apparently silly pricing policies may well have economic theory on their side – and Mr Becker outside queueing to get in.

[1]'A note on restaurant pricing and other examples of social influences on price.' By Gary Becker. *Journal of Political Economy*, October 1991.

Questions

1. Explain what is meant by 'market clearing'.

2. Explain what is meant by a 'Giffen good' and give an example.

3. What factors influence the demand for goods such as a Swatch?

4. What makes Swatch watches different? Why do other manufacturers make their products have the same characteristics?

5. Draw Gary Becker's demand curve and add supply curves to show the two equilibriums.

The Royal Game

If only there were more courts for commoners and princes to set the chase

NEXT week, at the splendid Racquet & Tennis Club on Manhattan's Park Avenue, either Wayne Davies will remain or Lachlan Deuchar will become one of sport's least-known world champions. Do not, however, assume a contest on a physical par with tiddlywinks: real tennis (meaning 'royal', rather than 'genuine', and also known as court tennis) is the finest racquet sport of all – as fast as squash, more subtle than lawn tennis, more athletic than racquets, more everything than America's racquetball.

Why, then, is it not popular? The uninitiated point to the complexity of the game. The service bounces along a sloping roof called the penthouse to a receiver at the 'hazard' end. The receiver can win a point by striking the ball across the sagging net into the 'dedans' at the server's end; the server can reply by either hitting the ball into the 'grille' at the receiver's end, or into the 'winning gallery' (which is festooned with bells to signal success). One added advantage for the server is the 'tambour', a deceptive side-wall angle on a right-handed receiver's backhand. As if that were not confusing enough, the players change ends by setting a 'chase' – far too complicated to explain, but allowing a

'realer' (ordinary tennis players are called 'lawners') to use the strategic thinking of a chess player. As this month's *Tennis World* wrote of the play-off match in Melbourne for the right to challenge Mr Davies: 'Deuchar hit four grilles and two winning galleries, served giraffes on short chases and thoroughly frustrated Snow's every effort.'

In fact, such esoterica are part of the game's charm. The true reason for its rarity is money. As Mr Deuchar says: 'It's an expensive game and there's no point saying otherwise.' For example, the racquet, with its lopsided head, is made from the wood of the ash tree and will cost around £80. Because of the ball – the size of a tennis ball but much heavier – a professional will go through 15 racquets in a year; an average club player perhaps two. That, however, is no more expensive than getting the equipment for squash or lawn tennis. The big difference is in paying for the court. When real tennis – which began as an 11th-century hand-ball played by French monks in cloistered courtyards – was truly royal, there were courts everywhere.

But then came revolution in France and social change in Britain. Today there are only three courts in France, four in

Australia (which provides many of the professionals, including Messrs Davies and Deuchar), nine in America and 20 in Britain. With perhaps 5,000 players, demand is rationed by stiff club fees and long waiting-lists.

The obvious answer should be to build new courts. But a real tennis court is as large as a three-storey house. To build such a court might cost well over $350,000; servicing the debt, maintaining the facilities and paying a professional could mean at least $100,000 a year, to be extracted from a maximum number of players per court of 200. Investors who look at 'opportunity cost' prefer to build squash courts – or aerobics centres.

Happily, not everyone is transfixed by such simple arithmetic. In 1989 the Oratory School, a Roman Catholic boarding school deep in rural Berkshire, opened a sports centre featuring a real tennis court. Next month Chelsea's new Harbour Club will open the first real tennis court to be built in London this century – with Mr Deuchar as its professional.

With only three other courts in London, the same may prove true for the Harbour Club. Many sports are addictive, but unlike squash, with its heart-breaking stress, or racquets, with its need for a brilliant eye, real tennis is a habit that can be indulged even by octogenarians. Moreover, because guile comes with experience and because a handicapping system was introduced in 1981, the old can also beat the young. All of which helps explain a recent lengthening of the waiting-lists.

The question is whether popularity will provoke change in a sport whose professionals still make the balls by hand. In 1991 an Australian company produced a prototype graphite racquet. Fortunately, the controlling Tennis and Rackets Association, based at Queen's Club in London, had no wish to encourage real-tennis equivalents of Boris Becker and Goran Ivanisevic. It banned grap-hite. The result is that real tennis remains the most varied of games, with dozens of differents serves, volleyed returns and sliced half-volleys. Best of all, the ball still comes off the strings with the sweetness of a David Gower (cricket) drive through the covers.

Side-bets apart (the top amateur, Britain's Julian Snow, is a great betting man), real tennis players earn precious little money to make up for their lack of fame. A typical prize for the world championship, for example, is a mere £10,000, which compares with £3,975 for a man who loses in the first round at Wimbledon. But you will still not hear the world champion next month wishing he had been a 'lawner' instead of a 'realer'.

Questions

1. Explain what is meant by 'opportunity cost'. What is the opportunity cost of building a real tennis court? Of answering this question?

2. Draw a demand and supply diagram and then shift the curves to increase the quantity. What factors do you think would cause these curves to shift in the case of real tennis?

3. Use demand and supply analysis to explain why you think that real tennis champions in tournaments earn so little.

Cool Costing

The price of changing global warming

NOBODY is sure how far and how fast the earth will warm up as carbon dioxide (CO_2) and other gases build up in the atmosphere. But that did not stop governments from signing a treaty last year to try to reduce the growth of such gases, nor economists from estimating the cost of the policies that the treaty may imply.

Most economists have looked at the economy of the United States, and extrapolated from that. But the OECD has a model which does better, and the findings so far are summarised in its latest *Economic Studies*. The model has two special features. It can look in some detail at individual regions, such as China, India or the EC, and at the trade flows between these regions. That allows it a unique view of how different policies would affect international competitiveness. It can also look at the ways energy prices are distorted by taxes and subsidies.

Some of the findings should cheer the officials who hope to turn last year's climate treaty into something workable. For instance, the OECD thinks that the cost of stabilising the global output of CO_2 at 1990 levels by 2050 would be between 1% and 3% of world GDP. That (to pessimists)

means forgoing the entire output of Canada today; but (for optimists) it is only one year's world economic growth.

Setting aside the question of whether such a cost would buy commensurate benefits (which the OECD has not yet tried to answer), any agreement should aim to be as cost-effective as possible. That implies reducing CO_2 output in the countries where it is cheapest to do so, rather than sharing cuts equally across the board. The most cost-effective places to make cuts turn out to be the coal-producing developing countries, which means mainly China and India. The alternative – brave gestures by the rich countries to reduce their own CO_2 output – will have little effect on the global total, because of the rate at which energy use by the non-OECD countries is likely to grow.

The way a carbon-cutting agreement is designed will determine which countries carry most of the cost. But, as the OECD shows, no agreement will work unless the countries that are likely to cut least (the OECD nations) are willing to make large payments to compensate those that cut most (the big third-world energy producers). The most heartening finding of the OECD's work is

how much the growth of CO_2 output could be cut without making any country worse off. This is largely due to the amount of subsidy slopping around in the system. Domestic energy prices in many countries outside the OECD have been hugely subsidised. Energy subsidies, net of taxes, cost the world $235 billion in 1985. The effect is to underwrite CO_2 output. In non-OECD countries, the implicit carbon subsidy worked out at $90 a tonne in 1985, the equivalent of $10 a barrel of oil. Removing those subsidies will make their economies work more efficiently – and reduce their output of global-warming gas.

What if global warming turns out to be less sinister than most scientists now think, or if last year's convention is stillborn? Will all this high-powered economics be no more than intellectual calisthenics? The work on energy subsidies will still be useful. Indeed, it has already helped to transform the World Bank's approach to energy use in developing countries and especially in the former Soviet Union. Energy use, and particularly coal, does plenty of much less controversial environmental harm. And energy subsidies do uncontroversial economic damage.

Questions

Note: 'OECD' is the Organization for Economic Cooperation and Development, an association of the richer countries of the world.

1. Explain how 'energy prices are distorted by taxes and subsidies'.

2. Show how 'energy subsidies do uncontroversial economic damage'.

3. Why does the author argue that cuts should be made in the coal-producing developing countries such as China or India? What counterarguments could the governments of these countries make?

4. The UK government introduced taxes on fuel in 1994. Find out what effect this has had on fuel use (from some source such as *Economic Trends*), and comment on your findings.

The Fall of Big Business

CORPORATE giants once walked tall and proud, bestriding the globe, champions of this century's miraculous economic growth. The goal of every ambitious company was to join them and, like them, be mighty enough to shrug off the blows which regularly toppled smaller rivals.

But these are troubling times for the world's biggest companies. Their presumption of invincibility is now in shreds. Spectacular failures at General Motors, IBM and Philips, once paragons of business success, have shown big firms to be frighteningly vulnerable to changes in their markets and to economic downturns. Hundreds of other big firms, from Japan's Matsushita to Germany's Daimler–Benz, are struggling to refashion themselves to avoid a similar fate.

The humbling of big firms has only just begun. Economic recovery will offer some respite, but not much. In a broad range of industries, powerful forces are moving against big companies. New technology has spread around the world, trade barriers have come down, financial markets have been deregulated and consumer tastes have converged across borders. All these changes were once expected to give big

firms even more scope to flex their muscles. Instead they have granted business opportunities to thousands of small and medium-sized companies, and shown the bodies of many corporate behemoths to be mostly flab. As these trends accelerate, the crucial question facing the managers of large companies will be not how their firms can grow bigger still, but whether they can survive without shrinking.

When globalisation became a cliche, businessmen assumed that big firms would gain the most from lower trade barriers and converging tastes. Global markets, it seemed, would call for global brands from global companies managed globally. Firms big enough to spend lavishly on automated factories and computerised offices would be able to exploit glittering new technologies faster than smaller, and poorer, rivals. Increasingly sophisticated and deregulated capital markets would enable big firms (but only big firms) to scour the world for the cheapest money. Many pundits confidently forecast that a handful of giant firms would dominate car making, electronics, banking, entertainment, publishing and advertising, to name only a few.

At the time such predictions seemed plausible. For decades firms in almost every business had sought 'economies of scale' - the idea that manufacturing or distributing goods in ever larger volumes lowers costs per unit, so that a firm becomes more efficient as it grows. Most managers recognised that expanding a business also involves new costs. As they grow, firms may become bureaucratic, inflexible and wasteful. Employees, believing themselves to be mere cogs, are less accountable and harder to motivate.

Far from presenting the world's biggest companies with new opportunities, falling trade barriers are opening them to attack.

The difficulties of operating in dozens of countries may have annoyed big firms, but they were often the only companies able to surmount such obstacles. Few small firms could afford to tailor their products to the standards of foreign markets, employ people overseas or cope with the legal and tax complexities of international business.

The opening of markets is removing many of these barriers and making it easier for smaller firms to sell their products all over the world. Another blow to big firms is that the use of computers, confounding most forecasts, is narrowing economies of scale in manufacturing and distribution, not expanding them. Factory automation is making it possible to produce goods cheaply in much smaller volumes. The plummeting price of computers is enabling smaller firms to employ the same logistical techniques, sophisticated financial models, and automated payrolls and other administrative tasks that were available only to big firms in the past.

Other trends are pushing the same way. The growing efficiency and internationalisation of capital markets is allowing medium-sized firms to raise money in much the same way as the world's biggest companies. Consumer tastes are converging as predicted but, entranced by greater choice, consumers are also becoming more fickle. And the quality-control techniques pioneered in Japan are being applied almost everywhere by big and small firms alike, eliminating any variation in the

quality of many products. Both changes are beginning to erode the power of established brands, the most precious assets of giant consumer-product companies such as Philip Morris, Procter & Gamble or Unilever. Similarly, bigger firms can still spend bigger sums on R&D, but in an embarrassing number of industries, from computers to biotechnology, small and medium-sized firms are proving the most innovative.

As the advantages of corporate gigantism diminish, its long-ignored costs are becoming painfully evident. Many large firms are scrambling to reduce these, scrapping layers of middle managers, cutting overheads and reorganising themselves into 'federations' of autonomous business units – that is, they are trying to become more like their smaller rivals. They are also increasingly wary of becoming yet bigger, choosing joint ventures and alliances as the way into new markets, rather than following the earlier path of buying other firms.

These are steps in the right direction. But as the pressures on the world's biggest firms grow, their shareholders will have to take more drastic action, and in many cases consider that most dreaded of corporate taboos: the break-up. There will be exceptions, such as the commercial-aircraft industry, where the financial barriers to entry will remain formidable, and where big companies will prosper. In most other industries, however, 'economies of scale' will be achieved at much smaller volumes than before. In other words, if markets are left alone, in many industries the optimal size of companies will shrink. As this happens, consumers can only benefit. The vision of small groups of massive firms towering over world markets never held much promise for them. But for managers, life will be much tougher. The era of corporate empire-building is over. An age of broader, fiercer global competition, with all its risks and uncertainties, has begun.

COPYRIGHT © THE ECONOMIST NEWSPAPER LIMITED, LONDON (APRIL 1993)

The Essence of the Story

- Large firms were once admired, but recently many large companies have fallen on difficult times. Changes such as the fall in trade barriers, technological innovation and converging consumer tastes were expected to favour giant companies, but the beneficiaries have been small and medium-sized firms.

- The opening of international markets has removed many barriers to trade and made it easier for small and medium-sized firms to sell their products abroad.

- Computers have brought economies of scale to smaller companies and the internationalization of capital markets makes it easier for medium-sized firms to raise capital.

● These changes have caused large firms to reorganize and in many cases shareholders have advocated breaking up large firms and selling off particular parts.

Background and Analysis

Marxist economists believe that there is an inevitable move to greater concentration of industrial power as large firms gobble up their smaller competitors.

Other economists also note the importance of large firms; for example in 1991 Shell had a turnover of £52,000 million.

One reason for the existence of large firms is the existence of economies of scale. Sometimes these accrue to the plant or factory. Examples are the benefits arising from the division of labour and the ability to use specialized machinery.

Some economies of scale accrue to the firm; for example the ability to borrow money more easily and cheaply. Large firms can also afford to spend more on research and development and may have marketing economies – an advert for Heinz beans also benefits other Heinz products.

Non-technical economies of the firm	Optimum number of cars per year
Advertising	1,000,000
Sales	2,000,000
Risks	1,800,000
Finance	2,500,000
Research and development	5,000,000

Source: adapted from Dunnett, P.J.S., *The Decline of the British Motor Industry*, Croom Helm (1980)

As the table shows, there is evidence to suggest that in manufacturing there are still considerable economies of scale.

The article suggests that this position may be changing, causing firms to reorganize. There is certainly some evidence to support this line of argument, and a number of large firms have sold off subsidiaries.

However, it is also possible that the problems of large firms are not caused solely by the changes described in the article, but arise from the recession which has led large firms to cut staff and change their management structures.

Questions

1. Explain with examples what is meant by 'economies and diseconomies of scale'.

2. Summarize the arguments in the article which suggest that economies of scale are less important than they used to be and are achievable at lower levels of output. Can you think of any counterarguments?

3. Look up statistics to see if the largest firms (for example, the five largest firms in an industry) are more or less important than they were a decade or so ago. (You can find this information in many introductory texts, or in books on industrial economics. In a large library, information on size of firms can be found in *Business Monitor PA 1002*.)

Taking GM Apart:

A disposal for General Motors?

Could General Motors be plotting a de-merger for its giant components business

RUMOURS are rife in motor city of a plan to hive off its Automotive Components Group (ACG). With sales to GM and some 30 other car companies of almost $25 billion in 1993, ACG is the world's biggest components group – twice the size of Germany's Robert Bosch. Strategically, a de-merger would take GM a big step closer to the sort of structure most other car companies already have.

GM is vertically integrated to an unusual extent. Thanks to ACG, the GM group makes 65–70% of the parts used in its cars. In contrast, Ford makes about 50% of its parts and Chrysler only 30%. Japanese car makers produce even fewer of their own parts, though they enjoy close links with the parts suppliers. 'In a perfect world, GM's managers would like nothing better than to wake up tomorrow with an in-house supplier providing about 25% of their parts,' says Maryann Keller, an analyst at Furman Selz and an author of two books on the company.

When Jack Smith took over as boss of the troubled giant in 1992 he made no secret of his desire to shed

peripheral businesses. But Mr Smith and his colleagues have found it hard going: they have so far backed away from the sale of one business that makes railway engines, another that makes transmission systems for tanks and a third that sells home loans. None attracted the prices GM wanted.

For many years, ACG has been trying to become less dependent upon its parent. GM is now freeing its assembly plants to buy from the cheapest suppliers they can find, anywhere in the world. This increases the pressure on ACG. The group has been reorganised and loss-making units are being sold off. An over-extended product line has been streamlined into a range of basic systems, run by seven divisions with names such as Delco Chassis, Delco Remy, Packard Electric and AC Rochester, which have been revered in the industry for decades. The group says it lost over $500m in 1991, but that opening profits in 1993 could exceed $1 billion.

ACG's executives have been busy telling industry conferences about their growing independence from

GM. The subsidiary has also begun to form joint ventures with other suppliers. These include a $500m venture with ITT Auto, to manufacture small electric motors. ACG expects its non-GM sales to go on growing at 10–12% a year, compared with 2–3% for sales to its parent. Even then, however, non-GM sales are unlikely to rise to more than 30% of the total within a few years.

That degree of dependence could make it hard to find a buyer for the parts maker. So one approach might be to turn ACG into a wholly owned subsidiary affiliated with a specific class of GM stock. This would put it in the same category as EDS, a computer-services company, and Hughes Electronics, two other businesses owned by GM. That would help to strengthen ACG's independent image. It would not, though, do much for its parent's deepest problems, such as its vast health-care costs, an unfunded pension liability of $24 billion and hopelessly uncompetitive labour costs – including those incurred in ACG's factories.

Nowadays, there are few easy solutions for GM.

Questions

1   Explain what is meant by 'de-merger', 'vertically integrated' and 'wholly owned subsidiary'. Give another example of vertical integration.

2. Find out what products are made by General Motors (for example, from their annual report). What economic advantages and disadvantages does this wide range of products have for a company?

3. Why do you think General Motors would like to de-merge its components group?

4. Find out how Japanese firms organize production (from any book on industrial economics). What advantages does this give to firms?

The Price of Competition

New entrants into gas, power and telephone markets often have to use monopolists' pipes and wires. How much should they pay for the privilege?

MONOPOLY is not what it used to be. Least of all, perhaps, for utilities, such as gas, electricity and telephone companies. Until recently, few believed that they would be exposed to competition. Now Americans, Britons and New Zealanders can choose their telephone company. By 1998 British households will be able to shop around for electricity; big firms already can.

But there is a snag. New competitors need pipes or wires to reach their customers. It is inefficient to build new ones. And existing networks are usually owned by the utilities with which the newcomers want to compete. Left to themselves, incumbents could keep new rivals out by denying them access or by quoting a price so high that they go away. So regulators have to intervene to see fair play.

One solution is to force utilities to split their businesses between network operations and the supply of final products – either through full divestment or by some less drastic means, such as having separate accounts for each bit. This should cut out much jiggery-pokery: a network operator with no presence in the market for final products has no interest in keeping others out.

But it may not always be for the best. Britain's electricity industry has undergone separation with some success, and its gas market may follow. But curbs on America's telephone companies, such as the ban on them supplying cable TV, may have restricted competition.

An alternative is to control the prices paid for access to networks. But this is a thorny task. The usual economists' mantra that prices should equal marginal cost (i.e., the costs imposed on the network by the last kilowatt, therm or phone call carried) is of little use. Because they have big fixed costs, networks enjoy economies of scale: marginal-cost pricing would leave the network owner out of pocket.

The usual way around this has been to recover fixed costs by bumping up charges for using the network – for instance at times of heavy demand. Most American regulators have adopted such a rule; British Gas and its regulator are discussing one. Economists tend to see it as a necessary evil. Because such prices differ from marginal costs, they do not give firms the right market signals. But some sacrifice of efficiency may be needed to cover costs.

In a forthcoming book[1]

two American economists, William Baumol and Gregory Sidak, say that regulators should tear up their traditional rules. Marginal-cost pricing, they say, is the right way to go. The trick is to redefine the marginal cost to the network owner of providing access. This consists of more than just extra wear and tear on the system. Because the network owner is also in the market for the final product, it will lose revenues to any newcomer. The prices that regulators let the network owner charge for final products also make a contribution to the network's fixed costs. In losing market share to newcomers, the network owner loses this contribution, which Messrs Baumol and Sidak call an 'opportunity cost'; they say it should be included in the access price.

Such an approach – dubbed 'efficient component pricing' (ECP) – appears to do four clever things. First, it sends the right signals to new suppliers about whether or not they should enter the market. If a newcomer can make the final product more cheaply than an incumbent, it can make a profit by renting the network. Second, the technique ensures that network costs are covered. Third, it means that utilities should worry less about entrants 'cream-skimming' customers located in the lucrative bits of the network (such as city centres), who often cross-subsidise other bits. And fourth, it implies that there is no need to separate the network from the supply of final products: faced with the right access prices, incumbents should have no incentive to keep rivals out.

Some regulators agree. America's railway regulator has adopted ECP in some disputes over rail-track prices. California's telephone watchdog has done the same. And last December New Zealand's High Court said ECP should be applied to the telephone network – although that decision is now under appeal.

Is ECP too good to be true? One criticism is that by requiring entrants to reimburse utilities for lost revenues, ECP looks like a monopolist's charter. Not so, say Messrs Baumol and Sidak. The regulated final-product price, they argue, should mimic the outcome in a 'contestable' market – one with no barriers to entry. If regulation is slack, so that final prices are too high and access prices are driven up, that does not invalidate ECP. Fair enough: but accurate price-setting is a tough business.

Defining 'opportunity cost' is another problem. If the market has a fixed number of customers, with the result that all of a new entrant's sales are poached from the incumbent utility, it is fairly easy. But if the entrant's product differs from, or is cheaper than, the incumbent's, the market will expand. Working out what the monopolist has forgone is then much trickier. Mr Baumol agrees. But in practice, he says, the scope for argument about access charges is still less than in conventional network pricing.

So does ECP help? It is a good framework in which to think about the price of network access. But regulators should beware. ECP still leaves them with a lot of work to do. They still need to get the control of final prices right. And they still need to decide what 'opportunity cost' means in practice. Neither is easy.

[1]Toward Competition in Local Telephony', W. Baumol and G. Sidak, MIT Press and the American Enterprise Institute, 1994.

Questions

1. What is a 'natural monopoly'? Give examples.

2. Explain with examples what is meant by opportunity cost. How is this concept used in this article?

3. Explain why utilities do not usually face competition.

4. Why do economists suggest that price should equal marginal cost? Why is it suggested that this policy is unworkable?

5. Summarize the proposals concerning 'efficient component pricing'. What problems does this seek to overcome? What problems does it cause?

Monopoly Prophets

What the world's privatisers can learn from Britain's disposal of its state-owned utilities

IT WAS once the fashion to sneer at Britain's obsession with privatisation. Nowadays the whole world is putting its state-owned companies up for sale, just as Britain did in the 1980s. Governments from Latin America to the ex-communists of Eastern Europe are being no less radical than was Margaret Thatcher. Indeed, the state enterprises currently heading for the marketplace include the politically sensitive telephone, energy and transport companies once considered particularly unsuited to private ownership. As natural monopolies, it was said, these utilities could not be sold off in a way that would bring the benefits of competition to bear. Yet Britain went ahead and did it anyway.

Now that the rest of the world is following Britain's lead, Britons themselves are having second thoughts. It is not so much the principle of privatising utilities that is being questioned – even the Labour Party is squeamish about taking back what has already been sold – but the manner in which the privatised companies are subsequently regulated. That they need regulation is clear: somebody has to prevent a private owner of a natural monopoly from awarding himself monopoly profits.

The American approach tends to be legalistic: strict rules are laid down for regulated companies to follow. Another way would have been political: to make the newly privatised companies directly accountable to parliament or to a government ministry. Britain chose to steer between these alternatives. It gave the job to an independent regulator with plenty of discretion. Too much discretion, say the critics. Both the companies themselves and some independent academics complain that the British system is unpredictable, because it depends too much on the idiosyncrasies of individual regulators. It is accused of being too hard on some utilities and – worse – too soft on others. British Gas has lowered its prices by 20% in real terms since privatisation in 1986 (while its bosses have personally fallen out with the regulator); electricity prices have increased by 4% since 1990. While one regulator takes a dim view of environmental measures, another demands them. While the electricity regulator declines to tamper with the formula setting prices, the water regulator has kept the formula, but revised prices all the same. The uncertainty of all this, the critics argue, is unjust and expensive.

Is there a case for an overhaul? On its own, conflict between the regulator and the regulated is not conclusive evidence that the system does not work; it would indeed be suspicious if a would-be monopolist got on famously well with the person responsible for restraining his profits. Besides, the full evidence on Britain's experiment is not yet in. Those who argue that regulators of telecoms and gas have been tough, whereas those of water and electricity are weak, should remember that neither of the softies has yet conducted his first five-year review of the price formula: this will be the real test of the newer regulators' mettle.

The charge that cannot be evaded is that the British system depends too much on personal whim. Much of this arises from mistakes made when the utilities were privatised. Not all the elements of a utility need to be monopolies: in electricity, for example, distribution is likely to be a monopoly but generation is not. British Gas and BT were kept too large for competition to emerge, except with the regulators' help. In both industries, elements of the nationalised monopoly were left in place. Thus the regulators had not only to shoulder an unnecessary burden of regulation, but also to decide how far to distort the market in order to encourage competition.

So the first lesson from Britain is to get the structure of the industry right from the very beginning: wherever there is room for competition, it is preferable to regulation. But where a regulator is needed, his independence must be tempered by accountability – especially to consumers. Britons need an easier route of appeal over the heads of individual regulators to their national competition authority. That done, the British system may still be better than its alternatives. It has long been argued that the greatest threat to any system is 'regulatory capture'. Political regulators have been subverted by the lobbying of big industries. Legalistic regimes have bent under the weight of a regulated industry's superior resources, which have given it the edge when decisions are challenged in the courts. Independence – within limits – is the best defence against this sort of capture.

Questions

1. Explain what is meant by 'natural monopoly' and 'monopoly profit' and show how unregulated natural monopolies can earn monopoly profits.

2. What reasons do you think the writer could have put forward to support the assertion that competition is better than regulation?

3. Find out how regulators control natural monopolies (for example from an introductory economics text or a book on industrial economics). What criticisms does the writer make of such regulation?

4. Find out how Ofgas is seeking to replace regulation with competition in the UK gas market. (A CD-ROM search or the report of the regulator will give this information.) Who will benefit and who will lose from this change?

Who's Afraid of the MMC?
Competition policy

IN the heyday of Thatcherism, competition was the Tories' big gun in their battle against industrial decline. The troika of the Department of Trade and Industry (DTI), the Monopolies and Mergers Commission (MMC) and the Office of Fair Trading (OFT) had a mission to seek out and destroy monopolies wherever they lurked.

Not so now. Ambitious plans to strengthen the OFT have come to nothing. And now there is a growing unease in many quarters about the performance of the MMC: has it gone soft? The main worry concerns the MMC's monopoly-bashing role. A series of recent MMC reports, say critics, have shown too much respect for the views of the firms under investigation. In 1991 monopolies in photocopiers, instant coffee and soft drinks were all left largely intact. A report on the prices charged by BAA, an airports operator, sidestepped important questions about the future of duty-free sales and whether BAA should be broken up. And last month a report on the sale of motor cars that was widely expected to reshape the industry did no more than tinker with it. Contrast this with the heady days of the late 1980s, when the MMC helped to liberalise industrial-gas supply and aimed to weaken the control that brewers had over pubs.

Much of this criticism is harsh. Ever since an earlier industry secretary, Norman Tebbit, narrowed the definition of 'public interest' to the effects of a monopoly or merger on competition, the MMC has at least taken a more consistent line on takeovers. And none of the recent reports has been easy; economists differed sharply over some of the questions that needed confronting. (Some disagreements have still not been satisfactorily resolved: the break-up of brewing, though based on well-argued economics, is now widely viewed as a disaster.) Perhaps complaints about the MMC simply come from aggrieved parties? Any worthwhile monopoly investigation, after all, is likely to leave behind disgruntled losers.

The car report suggests there is more to it than that. The investigation behind it, the longest and costliest ever done by the MMC, went to extraordinary lengths to give carmakers a chance to colour the arguments in their favour. For instance, an independent report that showed huge differences in prices between cars sold in Britain and in continental Europe was sent out to manufacturers for 'consultation'; the numbers used in the final report showed a much smaller gap. And this gap was explained away by some shoddy economics. It was noted that cars sold in Britain tended to have extra 'add-ons', for example, and that the price differential got smaller when these were taken into account; but these add-ons were valued at manufacturers' retail prices, not at what they actually cost. By contrast, the European Commission is expected soon to take a far tougher line towards the motor industry.

Of course, the car report may be a one-off lapse. But the MMC's critics fear it may have taken too much to heart the government's fudge over the brewing industry. On that occasion, heavy lobbying by the industry prompted the then industry secretary, Lord Young, to back away from crucial proposals from the MMC. Did the commission see this as a signal from the government that radical solutions would no longer be welcome? (Much of the subsequent mess over brewing, incidentally, reflects the legacy of Lord Young's compromise, rather than the contents of the original MMC report.) Another problem is the growing number of firms taking the MMC to court. Several recent cases have been subjected to judicial review; though the MMC has won most of them, the prospect of long legal battles may be instilling an undue caution.

The success of utility regulation may offer some clues as to how the MMC might be improved. Regulators like Oftel and Ofgas are independent of politicians, have clear duties and are supplemented by the role of the MMC as a 'court of appeal'. If the regulator and a utility cannot agree, the dispute can be referred to the MMC. Contrast this with how other monopolies are regulated: the OFT asks the MMC to investigate, the MMC makes recommendations to the industry secretary, and the secretary does as he pleases.

Why not bestow on the OFT a duty to promote competition, together with powers to investigate and to make rulings? A parallel reform could establish the MMC as an independent, quasi-judicial body – rather than the collection of part-time businessmen and academics who currently make up the commission. Only if firms were unhappy with the OFT's decision would the MMC be involved; the industry secretary would play no part at all. Turning the MMC into a 'court of appeal' in this way would also make it harder for companies to tie up the new-style OFT in lengthy and costly litigation.

Today's OFT is inflexible and slow, often busying itself with insignificant cases while failing to deal with serious anti-competitive agreements. The 1989 white paper on restrictive trade practices made a powerful case for reform, which time has done nothing to dilute. Its recommendations were to strengthen the OFT's investigative powers, bring British rules into line with those of the European Commission and allow offending firms to be fined up to £1m.

Questions

1. Explain the work of the OFT and the MMC.

2. Why do we need such bodies?

3. Find any MMC report and comment on its recommendations.

4. Compare and contrast UK and EU competition policies.

Pleasing Nobody

The EC's competition policy

IS THE European Commission the right body to run the European Community's antitrust policy?

The authors of the Community's founding Treaty of Rome thought so 35 years ago, when they put antitrust in the commission's hands to keep it away from national politicians. But the creation of a single European market has turned the commission itself into a political battleground, and many of the fiercest battles have been over competition policy.

A series of controversial decisions by Sir Leon Brittan, the competition commissioner, and a handful of botched court cases have increased support for a separate antitrust authority independent of both the commission and national governments. The Treaty of Rome gives the commission the authority to crack down on price-fixing, cartels and other anti-competitive behaviour by firms that operate across the Community's national borders, and to ban government subsidies that distort trade. Since September 1990 the commission has also had the power to veto large cross-border mergers and takeovers.

As firms and governments have jostled for advantage in the emerging single market, the whole subject of competition regulation has become

fraught. In the most recent case, the German government wrote an angry letter to the commission about its decision to allow Alcatel, a French telecoms firm, to take over AEG Kabel, part of the Daimler–Benz group. German officials, saying they were not properly consulted, complain that the case, which will give the merged company 52% of the German market for some types of cable, should have been referred to Germany's own independent competition authority, the federal cartel office.

This is the second time in three months that a commission decision in favour of French firms has provoked howls. Last November the commission allowed Credit Lyonnais, a state-owned bank, to invest FFr2.5 billion in Usinor Sacilor, a state-owned steel maker. German and British steel makers were furious, complaining that the investment was a disguised government subsidy. Some lawyers in Brussels wonder whether the commission is trying to be nice to France because some earlier decisions had produced similar French outrage. These included the commission's demand that Renault, a state-owned car maker, repay money given to it by the French government in 1990; and the commission's veto in October of a

joint takeover of De Havilland, a Canadian aircraft maker, by France's Aerospatiale and Italy's Alenia, both state-owned firms.

The De Havilland case split the commission, pitting Sir Leon against Martin Bangemann, the industry commissioner, who supported the merger. Mr Bangemann not only openly criticised Sir Leon's decision, but also complained that consultation procedures within the commission were inadequate. These were made more explicit last month, and now require Sir Leon to follow a detailed set of rules before making a decision on mergers. Sir Leon suffered another setback last month, when the European Court of Justice overturned two of his more controversial decisions on technical grounds. One required British Aerospace to return £44m in cash 'sweeteners' it had received from the British government in 1988 to buy Rover, a state-owned car maker. The other required the Dutch government to allow courier firms to compete with the country's postal monopoly. On March 11th a determined Sir Leon announced that he would launch yet another investigation of the payment to British Aerospace.

Since Sir Leon has had to wheel and deal to get his decisions past his fellow commissioners, and has had several of those decisions criticised, support has grown for an independent agency to rule on competition cases. It might be like Germany's cartel office, which in recent years has had only one of its decisions reversed by the German government. Located away from Brussels, the agency would publish its decisions before submitting them to the commission for approval. If the commission overturned an agency decision, it would have to explain publicly why it did so. The idea would be to make it far more difficult for politicians to meddle in competition issues. In a speech on March 5th, Sir Leon opposed the idea. He used the odd argument that the rest of the Community lacks the maturity to make a German-style independent agency work.

Questions

1. Explain what is meant by 'price-fixing', 'cartel', 'merger' and 'takeover' and give examples of the last two.

2. How do government subsidies distort trade?

3. Why do you think the EU needs an antitrust policy when individual governments have such policies?

4. Find out what powers on monopoly policy the Treaty of Rome gives the EU.

5. Consider the advantages and disadvantages of an independent EU body to investigate monopoly.

PART C: FACTORS OF PRODUCTION, DISTRIBUTION OF INCOME

The Rules of Attraction

Does your physical appearance affect your earnings?

MEN are forever moaning about the time and money women spend slapping on make-up, dieting and shopping for clothes. Yet, according to two new studies by American economists, it is a worthwhile investment: looking good yields big financial returns. Susan Averett and Sanders Korenman[1] have examined the link between pay differentials and weight for 23–31-year-olds, after adjusting for differences in social class. The hourly wage of fat women is, on average, 20% lower than the pay of a woman of average weight. But slimmers be warned: underweight women also take home slimmer pay-packets than average women do.

However, skinny women make up for this in the marriage market: they marry men with the highest earnings.

Husbands of skinny women earn on average 45% more than those of fat ones. Men, it seems, are different. Underweight men take home by far the lowest earnings, while slightly overweight men enjoy the fattest pay-packets – 26% more than their underweight colleagues.

A second study by Daniel Hamermesh and Jeff Biddle[2] considers how workers' earnings are affected by their overall looks, rather than just their weight. The authors used household surveys from America and Canada, which along with information on earnings also included interviewers' ratings of the appearance of those they interviewed – from strikingly attractive to ugly. The job market clearly rewards beauty. Very attractive men and women enjoy hourly earnings about 5% higher than those with average looks, even after adjusting for factors such as education. Plain women earn 5% less than average lookers, plain men 10% less.

Can't think what to buy your husband for Christmas? Make-up, of course.

[1] 'The Economic Reality of The Beauty Myth', NBER working paper no. 4521.
[2] 'Beauty and the Labour Market', NBER working paper no. 4518.

COPYRIGHT © THE ECONOMIST NEWSPAPER LIMITED, LONDON (DECEMBER 1993)

Questions and Student Answers

1. Why do you think that appearance affects earnings?

By putting ourselves in the position of an interviewing employer we can determine why appearance may play a part in earnings as well as successful interview technique. As the majority would appear well dressed for the job interview, in order to maximize their chances of being employed, then it would serve likewise to do the same when negotiating salary.

The attractive and debonair in the job interview strike a chord with an employer before qualifications and ability are even reached. Smart and attractive gives the impression of health and vitality suggesting an extra ability or facet beyond experience or education.

Well argued. This image of health therefore means an extra reward may well be forthcoming on the premise of extra productivity or reduced costs to the firm for sick pay.

Clean and smart also suggest high standards which expressed through clean grooming may also mean their work will meet the same attention to detail; perhaps this person has high values and enjoys challenges essential to meet deadlines or doing unsupervised work.

This is an ingenious answer, though it doesn't answer all the points; for example why skinny women (who may be fit and attractive) earn less than average.

2. Can you relate these findings to the textbook theories of income determination? Do they suggest that the theories are wrong?

You don't really develop this point about imperfect markets. Income determination in the world of imperfect labour markets is based on the interaction of demand and supply and elasticity of supply which may change the earnings of labour.

The traditional theory of the firm assumes that firms aim to maximize profits, this is likewise for the labour theory of marginal productivity. Profit maximization will occur when the marginal cost of employing an extra worker is equal to the marginal revenue that the extra worker's output earns, thus MC of labour = MR of labour to maximize profits.

A useful summary of traditional theory. As more workers are employed, diminishing returns to labour will set in, and eventually marginal revenue from extra workers will fall to their marginal costs and at this point firms stop employing extra workers and profits will be maximized. This is shown at point A on the diagram. The shape of the MRP curve indicates diminishing returns to labour.

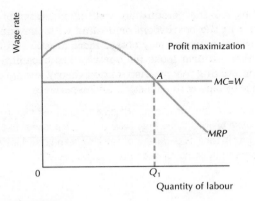

Figure 11.1

A perfectly inelastic curve shows that the wage rate makes no difference to the supply of labour. Is this true even for show business people? In order to affect the wage rate, labour must supply the correct skills to ensure higher earnings.

Education and training enhance a worker's status as does previous experience; a proven trade record may even overshadow qualifications in some occupations. By increasing their mobility and training workers can add extra power

This is not really linked to the argument about appearance.

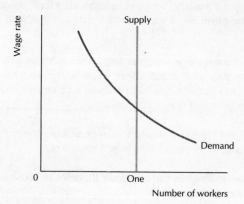

Figure 11.2

when supplying their skills in the labour market. The second diagram shows that supply of labour in this case is perfectly inelastic as only one worker is supplied, demand for labour determines the wage rate at point A. The diagram may relate to the situation a show business person may face for a person with unique talents, such as Red Adair, the oil fire expert in Kuwait during the Gulf war.

Clearly a link must be made between qualifications, training and our concern for appearance as a contributing factor to raise a person's market power and earnings. The value of appearance enhances a worker's market power and earnings. The value of appearance enhances market power to affect income determination just as education would as marginal benefit for that worker is raised by smart appearance. The textbook theories of income determination must surely allow for beauty in the labour market as well as mobility or experience.

A healthy looking person may well offer greater productivity on the factory floor, but in the boardroom or dealing with the public, a more rotund figure and physical presence may obtain more drastic results. Clearly, when employing workers, a firm looks for our physical capability alongside qualifications. Far from proving income distribution theory wrong, it can incorporate appearance side by side with education and experience.

You could use the evidence in the article to criticize traditional theory; for example, employers may not seek to maximize profits, they may have other objectives. In this case they may be willing to sacrifice some profit for the pleasure of working with good-looking people. This is a strong argument where the person appointing does not receive profits.

Suffer the Little Children's Goods

Making the rich feel good about child labour
may add to the wretchedness of the poor

IF A master finds, upon a short trial, that he can get enough work out of a boy without putting too much food into him, he shall have him for a term of years to do what he likes with.' Thus, with chilling brevity, does Charles Dickens explain the economics of child labour in 'Oliver Twist'; elsewhere he offers more painful detail. Much of the best of 19th-century literature, written amid the campaign to stop child labour in Britain, ensures that the West cannot forget that cruel business.

In time the West grew rich, and began to pass laws against the exploitation of children. In Britain, an act of 1920 made it illegal to employ anyone under the age of 14 full-time. In rich countries these days, only the voluntary bits of child labour survive: the bleary-eyed boy slogging round with the newspapers to earn a new bike, the car-washers with eager elbows and greasy cloths.

Not so in the poor world, where seven-year-olds still slave in factories, never learning, never playing, making carpets and clothes in the Indian subcontinent, leather goods in North Africa, all manner of stuff in Latin America. Nobody knows for sure how many children are in full-time work, but the International Labour Organisation believes that children account for up to 11% of the workforce in some countries in Asia, up to 17% in Africa and up to a quarter in Latin America.

Anybody with any humanity would like to see an end to this, and some humane people in the rich world are trying to do something about it. In America a bill is before the Senate Finance Committee that would allow the authorities, after an investigation to identify which industries in which countries use child labour, to ban the import of their goods unless the importer could produce a certificate to show that the goods had not been made by children. In Germany a large and loud lobby is agitating for something similar, and a voluntary labelling system is already being established so that products made without child labour get a stamp of approval.

These efforts sound blameless and benevolent. They make rich people feel better, which is not a reason to encourage them, though if it were their only by-product there would not be much cause to object. But it is not. First, child labour is being used as a pretext for protectionism by people who want to keep goods made by the poor out of the rich world's markets.

If a bit of protectionism were the price of ending child labour worldwide, few would balk. But protectionism is more likely to prolong it, which is part of the reason for the second argument against child-labour legislation: it would probably have an effect opposite to that which its sponsors say they intend. Suppose that the bill is passed, and a carpet factory that employs children can no longer export its products to America. The children thus put out of work will not be sent home, or to a well-stocked classroom: if they are prevented from working in an export industry, they will go to work in one that does not produce internationally traded goods. They will go into brick-making, or begging, or prostitution, or any of the myriad of opportunities open to the children of the very poor. This protectionism will marginally depress the export earnings of the country concerned, thus keeping it poorer for that much longer, depriving some future children of some of the benefits of development. The only country to benefit is the importing one, which appears to be helping the poor while actually slowing the economic growth of the country in which they live. It enjoys a warm glow of self-righteousness.

Child labour will not be

abolished by fiat, but by a combination of circumstances commonly known as progress. Most of the countries where children are widely employed have strict laws against their exploitation. But where parents are poor and education scarce, such laws tend to be flouted. In the meantime, the rich world does not have to import and do nothing. Contributing to the supply of primary education through aid organisations and charities would offer poor parents an incentive to keep their children out of factories for a few years in the hope of better-paid work later on. Such efforts can help children in poor countries; teaming up with protectionists to stop the poor getting richer will not.

Questions

1. Why do poor countries employ child labour? Why have richer countries limited it?

2. Summarize the views in the article about the effects which protectionism would have on child labour. Do you agree with this analysis?

3. What proposals would you make to reduce child labour in less developed countries?

Rich Man, Poor Man

The gap between high earners and the lowest paid has widened. Why?

ECONOMISTS have long sought ways to make the labour market work better: in particular, to encourage greater wage flexibility, so unemployed workers price themselves back into jobs. Since this implies a fall in pay at the lower end of the labour market, a good sign of an efficient job market (though, possibly, a socially divisive one) is a wide gap between the highest and lowest paid.

How does wage inequality vary between countries? And has the labour market been operating more flexibly in the past decade? The OECD provides some answers in its latest *Employment Outlook*. In the 1970s wage inequalities fell or were stable in most countries, but in the 1980s the gap widened in 12 of the 17 countries studied. America and Britain saw the biggest widening in wage differentials. In America the highest-paid 10% of workers earned 5.6 times as much as the lowest-paid 10% in 1989, up from 4.8 in 1980. In Britain the ratio increased from 2.5 to 3.4 in 1991. In most countries the wider dispersion of wages was attributable both to gains for high earners relative to median wages and to relative losses for the lower paid. The main exceptions were France and Germany where the wages of the low-paid rose relative to

average earnings. In America, Australia and Canada real wages for the bottom 10% of earners fell during the 1980s. In Britain, however, the real pay of the bottom 10% has risen by 11% since 1980 – albeit less than the 51% hike for the top 10%.

Why have wage inequalities widened in most countries? One possible explanation is the slew of labour-market reforms, such as decentralisation of wage bargaining, the move to performance-based pay, cuts in minimum wages and the decline in union power. The OECD reckons that such factors help to explain why America and Britain have seen the largest increase in wage inequality but cannot be solely responsible for the recent changes.

Another popular explanation for growing wage inequality, which many Americans fret about, is de-industrialisation: the replacement of 'high quality' jobs in industry by 'low quality' jobs in services, including the infamous hamburger-flipping 'McJobs'. The OECD study concludes, however, that shifts between different sorts of industry, such as between manufacturing and services, are much less influential than the changes within individual industries.

The most important causes

of increased wage differentials, says the OECD, are changes in the relative demand and supply of different types of workers, by age and by education. For example, most OECD countries saw a record number of 15 to 24 year olds enter the labour force in the 1980s. This reduced the wages for young workers relative to average wages, and so increased overall dispersion.

Perhaps the most striking increase in wage differentials was between workers with a university degree and those without. In the 1970s this gap narrowed as the supply of workers with a degree increased rapidly. In the 1980s, however, the supply of college-educated workers grew more slowly and their relative rewards rose. For example, in America the number of people with university degrees increased by an annual average of 2.6% in the 1980s, down from 4.4% in the 1970s. At the same time as the supply-growth of highly educated workers has slowed, the demand for them has accelerated. Techno-logical innovation – in particular, the increased use of computers – has added to the demand for highly educated, skilled workers and reduced the demand for less skilled. Putting these two factors together, the premium earned by

American university-educated workers over those who left after high school rose from 37% in the late 1970s to 53% in 1989.

The OECD thus rates education as one of the most important explanations for the increase in overall wage differentials. The more flexible a country's labour market, the more these changes in demand and supply show up in relative wages rather than unemployment.

Questions

1. Explain what is meant by 'real pay','performance-based pay', 'median earnings' and 'market clearing'.

2. Explain how 'unemployed workers can price themselves back into jobs'.

3. Use economic theory to explain why people with a degree earn more than those without and show how an increase in the supply of graduates can lead to a fall in their wage differentials.

4. Explain what is meant by 'de-industrialisation'. Why should this raise income inequality?

Big Brothers

Trade unions merge

MERGER mania has Britain's trade unions in its grip.

The unions should watch out. The arguments used for merger are horribly reminiscent of the big-is-beautiful corporate philosophy of the 1960s – and the mega-unions may ultimately prove as unsuccessful as mega-companies did then. Takeovers of failing unions by bigger ones were common in the 1980s. Some unions, particularly the multi-tentacled GMB, managed to maintain membership by judicious 'transfer of engagements' from smaller fry. Being takeovers, they have not caused serious problems.

But a new phase is under way: not the takeover of tiddlers but the merger of monsters. On July 1st, Unison, a combination of three public-service unions (NALGO, NUPE and COHSE), was launched with a membership of nearly 1.5m. It follows the merger earlier this year of the AEU and the EETPU electrical and engineering workers. Talks are on between the GMB and the other large general union, the TGWU, aimed at creating a beast with a quarter of total union membership.

The only certain benefit from all this is fewer ugly acronyms. The arguments closely parallel those used for corporate mergers. Merger reduces competition in the existing market for members, so the organisation is free to go after new markets. ('New markets' in the case of unions means the two-thirds of workers who are not union members at all.) Merger promises economies of scale. Overheads, such as expensive headquarters, can be shared. Negotiating power is pooled.

In theory. But merged unions, like merged companies, will experience destructive infighting. Unison, for example, will have to persuade its conservative ex-NALGO members among local-government officers that their interests are the same as ex-NUPE street-sweepers and school-cleaners. The new organisations will have to accommodate skilled workers who may despise their unskilled brothers. Workers in the private sector may resent paying taxes to sustain their public-sector members. The large unions are run in very different ways. For example, power in the GMB is concentrated at regional level; the TGWU is structured around individual industries. The two will be hard to reconcile.

Trouble too looms where two or more union bosses have to decide who is to be top dog, for example Unison is to have three general secretaries. Meanwhile, a damaging game of leftier-than-thou is being played between the GMB's John Edmonds, and Bill Morris of the TGWU, as they prepare to compete for the general secretaryship of their mega-union.

If national unions were vital, then such costs might have to be borne. But the national union is turning into an anachronism. Traditional pay bargaining is breaking up. The public sector, like the private sector before it, is moving away from national negotiations towards local deals. The corresponding union tactic should be de-merger. The basic unit of trade-union organisation would be the workplace. Besides pay, local unions would concentrate on sorting out individual grievances and protecting members against arbitrary management. The role of national unions would be cut, perhaps to something like that played by trade associations in business. But Britain's union barons will not abdicate until the merger alternative has been tried and failed.

Questions

1. To what extent do you think that the economies and diseconomies of scale which apply to firms also apply to unions?

2. Find out how union membership has changed over the past decade (for example,

from the *Employment Gazette*). Do you think that this explains the urge to merge?

3. Will the unions themselves gain or lose if they follow the pattern of pay bargaining and break up or de-merge?

Women on Top

Labour-market deregulation is helping to create new jobs – but not necessarily for the men thrown out of their old ones

'HI HO, HI HO, it's off to work we go...' chanted the seven dwarfs, as they left Snow White to tend the house, and, of course, to look pretty and vulnerable. These days, it's a fairy tale. The seven dwarfs sit at home, unemployed, lamenting the shortage of jobs for unskilled males. Snow White has no time for such things. She is off to work.

And so it is in the real world. The balance between the sexes in the labour markets of Western Europe and America has changed. Understanding why and how is a crucial first step towards framing an effective policy on unemployment. Women still account for a lamentably small share of senior jobs; but lower down the ladder, things are different. In Britain, the number of women in work has increased by 18% since the late 1970s, while male employment has fallen by 7%. Britain now has almost as many female employees as male ones, though many are part-timers. In America, too, women have taken the larger share of America's new jobs since the late 1970s. On current trends, a 'typical' worker in America and Britain will be a woman by early in the next century.

A main cause of this change is the shift from manufacturing to services. The demand for unskilled, manual labour has slumped: brains are more use than brawn in the new jobs being created in information technology, health, education and other services. This puts women and men on more equal terms than in manufacturing. And for many employers, women workers are a bargain. Often eager for part-time jobs that allow them to combine work with child-rearing, they are willing to work for less. And the flexibility of part-time hours lets firms use labour more efficiently. The rise in female employment is welcome – both for the new employees and for the economy as a whole. By and large, the new women workers are not taking jobs previously done by men; they are paying taxes and adding to output. Nonetheless, the slump in demand for unskilled labour and the influx of female workers have combined to depress pay for unskilled and part-time jobs.

Men are less willing to work for very low pay. They may prefer to work in the black economy, or live off welfare. Many of them (unlike the women who had hitherto worked in the home) may choose crime. For these reasons, their condition raises pressing questions for public policy. Also, the shift from male to female employment is often happening not within households but between them. In Britain, women are more likely to work if their husbands also have jobs. One reason is that an unemployed man may lose some of his benefits if his partner takes a job – even a low-paid, part-time job. So Britain has more two-earner households than before, but still too many no-earner households. This threatens to concentrate poverty in a wholly unemployed underclass. There is no better way to transmit poverty from generation to generation.

The standard remedies for unemployment are deregulation of the labour market (favoured by the right) and measures to spur demand in the economy (favoured by the left). Faced with the long-term unemployed, neither is much use. Further deregulation would create more jobs (a good enough reason to do it), but these would most probably not be taken by unskilled, long-term unemployed men. Encouraging flexibility in working hours will probably help women more than unskilled men. In much of Europe (though not in Britain), demand is needlessly weak, so there is a good case, too, for an easing of monetary policy. Like deregulation, this would create some jobs; also like deregulation, it would fail to do much for the long-term unemployed. The shift from manufacturing – where men traditionally sought unskilled work – is not a cyclical phenomenon. So a cyclical remedy – hastening recovery by stimulating demand – is beside the point.

The real problem is the mismatch between the skills and attitudes of long-term unemployed men and the jobs available. In addressing this, there should be two priorities. The first is to reform tax-and-benefit systems. Here, governments must grapple with a familiar dilemma: for the sake of incentives, benefits should not be withdrawn too quickly from claimants as they find work and their income rises; for the sake of economy in public spending, resources must be aimed at those who really need help. Sorting out the anomalies in tax-and-benefit systems – eg, making it easier for claimants to take part-time jobs without losing all their benefits – cannot be quick, easy or cheap. But nor is it impossible. Devising a properly integrated system – one that avoids inadvertent 'spikes' in implicit tax rates – is mainly a matter of simplifying over-complicated tax-and-benefit rules. It can be done.

The other priority is to invest more in education. For the unskilled, this is not mainly a matter of spending more on higher education or on retraining – desirable as such investments may be for other reasons. In Britain and other countries, many of the long-term unemployed are incapable of being trained because they left school lacking basic knowledge: without adequate literacy and numeracy, acquiring new skills is almost impossible. Adult remedial education therefore needs to be part of any strategy to help the unskilled unemployed. These are long-term solutions, you may say. You would be right. Unfortunately, there is no plausible short-term remedy for unskilled unemployment – and the best time to start work on long-term remedies is now.

Copyright © The Economist Newspaper Limited, London (December 1993)

Questions

1. Find out how the number of men and women in employment has changed over the past decade (from the *Employment Gazette* or a book on labour economics) and then summarize the arguments in the article which explain them. Do you agree with these arguments?

2. Explain how the tax-and-benefit system can contribute to unemployment.

3. Find out how much the average man and woman worker earns and then use economic theory to explain your findings.

4. Use supply and demand analysis to show the effects of improvements in basic educational skills.

PART D: GDP, STANDARD OF LIVING

The Value of Drudgery

Putting a price on housework

How large is a country's economic output?

Certainly much bigger than its gross domestic product (GDP), which excludes big chunks of activity. In particular GDP ignores the production of services within the home, such as cleaning, caring for children and decorating. This has the bizarre result that, if a man marries his cleaner, turning a paid employee into an unpaid housewife, then GDP falls instantly even though much the same work gets done.

A recent study by the OECD[1] confirms what every household drudge has always claimed – working at home is more valuable than it is believed to be by those who spend their time making the wheels of commerce and industry turn.

But how to put a value on it? There are two main methods. The first is to value the time spent doing housework using the person's wage in the formal economy, ie, the opportunity cost of his – or more likely her – time. The snag with this, however, is that it produces the ludicrous result that washing-up done by an investment banker is worth more than washing-up done by a nurse. The second method is to value that time at the wage rate of a maid. Doing this, the OECD concludes that the value of housework would add between one-third to one-half to the GDP of the five large countries which it studied.

The results seem a little odd. Australians work hardest in the home; the Germans, who are supposed to be hyper-neat, the least. The hours spent doing housework have fallen over the years as more women have taken paid jobs. But the value of housework has not necessarily dropped because productivity has been increased by blenders, dishwashers and the like. When unemployment rises, people spend more time doing up their homes. If governments included this in GDP, there would be fewer recessions.

[1] 'What is Households' Non-market Production Worth?' Ann Chadeau, OECD Economic Studies No. 18.

Questions and Student Answers

1. **Explain what is meant by 'Gross Domestic Product'. Use some publication such as *Economic Trends* to find the official figure for UK GDP.**

You should emphasize paid output.

Yes, this is the difference between GDP and GNP.

Gross Domestic Product is the most common measurement of the income of a country. It represented the total output of goods and services produced by the country in a year. It only measures the nation's income generated from resources within its own boundaries: the value of its goods and services. The value of GDP can be measured by three methods: the expenditure method, the income method and the output method. All methods should give the same value of GDP.

The value of GDP in the UK for 1995 is £710 billion.

Give the source of your statistics. You could also point out that GNP statistics always contain errors.

2. Why do you think that housework is not included in gross domestic product? What other economic activities are excluded?

This is one reason. The other is conceptual – GDP is concerned with the money economy, and this excludes housework. And the opportunity costs of all the housework in the country would be impossible to calculate.

Housework is not included in the Gross Domestic Product figures because of the sheer complexity of obtaining accurate statistics. The practical implications of attempting to measure such activities are obvious. Firstly, the question of how to put a value on such work arises. Secondly, how to calculate how much time someone puts into an activity which is often done in a piecemeal way – 10 minutes here, 20 minutes there. The practical limitations of trying to assess the economic value of non-financial activities is an arduous task.

Attempting to value economic activity such as housework could be done by using the concept of opportunity cost. The opportunity cost of this activity is the best alternative which has to be given up, that is, the sacrifice that the person makes in order to do housework. Placing a value on the alternative could be used to place a value on housework. The value of housework would be determined by marketable skills in the formal economy of the person doing it. So the value of housework done by a brain surgeon would be worth more than that done by a secretary.

Should this be unskilled?

Another method is to value it according to what the going market rate for a housekeeper or decorator or whatever activity is. However, skilled occupations such as cleaning are particularly exposed to changes in supply and demand. In a recession, if it were a completely deregulated market, wages would fall as demand falls and supply increases (a larger pool of unemployed). Regional variations in unemployment and skills result in different wage levels for the same job in different parts of the country. This makes placing a value on such work even more difficult.

You go into quite a bit of detail here, but fail to answer the second part of the question which requires some mention of D.I.Y. and so on.

3. What is meant by 'opportunity cost'? Can you use this concept to explain why the hours spent doing housework have fallen in recent years?

There is also an opportunity cost when output is paid.

To individuals it is the opportunity cost which is important. If someone is doing housework on an unpaid basis, they are sacrificing another activity (in particular earning money in the formal economy). Many women who previously undertook housework recognized this and so decided to take up paid jobs in the economy. As a result the number of hours spent on housework has declined. But at the same time, because more women are working either full- or part-time in paid employment, household incomes have risen and the prices of consumer products fallen resulting in increased use of dishwashers, etc. So this has had the effect of increasing productivity.

Good – the central point.

However, it is not true to say that activities which are unpaid, such as DIY, cleaning and housework, have no effect on GDP. Firstly, if people decide to withdraw or not enter the labour market, then supply is reduced and wages go up. An increase in wages would have a multiplier effect on the economy and increase GDP. Also any unpaid work also requires materials – in the case of DIY, paint, tools and so on – and will need to be purchased thus increasing GDP.

The last part of your answer is not really relevant.

Measuring Child Poverty

WHAT defines a country as poor? Not just its GDP per head, says UNICEF, the United Nations' agency for children, in 'The Progress of Nations', a report published on September 22nd. Those figures can be distorted by a small number of very rich people. A measure such as the death rate among children under five, UNICEF argues, can say as much about poverty – it reflects the wealth, schooling and living conditions of the parents – as crude income data.

UNICEF ranks countries by what it calls 'national performance gaps'. For various indicators of welfare, it compares what a country with a given income per head 'ought' – by world averages – to achieve with what it actually does. For example, in Vietnam you expect 168 children dead,

per 1,000 births, before age five; the reality is 52. Gap: 114. Only China and Sri Lanka rate highly on both scales. Jamaica – which schools as large a proportion of its children as the United States – outshines Latin America, where Cuba leads. Latin countries do badly on schooling even compared with Africans, given their income. Brazil and Mexico have the same incomes per head, but Brazil is far worse at keeping its children alive. In that respect, Asian countries – except Indonesia, Pakistan and Bhutan – do better than expected. Gulf states, such as Kuwait and United Arab Emirates, both with low crude rates of child death, nevertheless score badly, given their wealth.

The aim of the exercise, says James Grant, UNICEF's

director, is 'to help prod the laggards' into doing better. Other tables in the report show familiar – but still shameful – statistics, such as child immunisation against measles. America does far less of this (77%), for all its wealth, than many poor countries, such as North Korea (99%), China (95%) and Egypt (90%). There are some surprises: child malnutrition is more widespread in south Asia, says the report, than in Africa.

One doubt. GDP is measured using exchange rates. But use purchasing-power parity – based on what a currency can buy locally – and some countries, notably China, are richer, and so should meet higher expectations. So their actual performance is – as UNICEF recognises – less good than its tables suggest.

Questions

1. What limitations does GDP have as a measure of economic welfare?

2. Explain 'purchasing-power parity' and explain why using this concept would change the performance of countries such as China.

3. Why do you think that countries such as Vietnam and Cuba have fewer child deaths than GDP per head would predict?

Where to Live

Nirvana by numbers

Where would you most like to live? Romantic Paris? Or perhaps you yearn for sunny Sydney or a Swiss ski resort. Holiday memories loom large in such choices, but what if the decision were based purely on statistics?

WHEN Christopher Columbus or Captain Cook first set foot in foreign lands they were venturing literally into the unknown. Today's foreign travellers are rather better-briefed: dozens of international statistical manuals are packed with figures on matters such as wealth, weather and women's rights. For 22 countries, rich and poor, we examined over 30 indicators which sum up the economic, social, cultural and political aspects of life. Some countries' number-crunchers are more reliable and honest than others. Where official figures were unavailable, we guessed. We then added all the indicators together, to see which country scores highest. Our round-the-world statistical tour starts with economics. If all you want is affluence, then America is the country of your dreams, with a GDP per head of $22,130, followed closely by Switzerland. At the other extreme the average Indian has an income of only $1,150 (all figures for 1991, converted at purchasing-power parities).

Many rich countries, however, have sluggish growth compared with the newly industrialising countries. A faster-growing, poorer economy may offer greater opportunities to get rich quick. For example, China and South Korea have both grown by an average of more than 9% a year over the past decade – more than three times as fast as America. The exception is Hong Kong, which has both a high average income of $18,520 (well ahead of Britain's $16,340) and one of the fastest growth rates.

High rates of inflation can make everyday life very complicated. Unless you have a degree in advanced mathematics, avoid Brazil, where annual inflation has averaged 472% over the past decade – it is currently running at around 2,000%. Japan or Germany (where inflation has averaged 2%) are a safer bet.

Unemployment is something which some governments try to lie about. For example, Russia boasted an official jobless rate of only 0.8% of the workforce in 1992 – the lowest rate in the table. But independent estimates suggest that it is really 7–10%. Spain is more honest, admitting to the highest unemployment rate (18.4%) of the 22 countries.

Nobody likes the taxman, but in some countries he is greedier than others. Taxes accounted for no less than 75% of GDP in Brazil in 1991, in part because of the impact of hyperinflation on the tax system. Sweden has the second highest taxes, at 50% of GDP, almost double America's 27%. The Bahamas (5%) or Hong Kong (11%) are for those who wish to minimise their tax bill.

The richer the country the more props of modern life there will be – from fax machines to microwaves. But even among rich countries there are huge differences. Sweden tops the telephone league, with 68 lines for every 100 people. By comparison, Spain has only 32 – fewer than any other industrial economy. America has the most cars: 589 for every 1,000 people, more than twice as many as in Japan. If you loathe cars, head for China or India (only 2 per 1,000).

Lots of cars and dirty industries mean pollution such as carbon-dioxide emissions from industrial processes. America has the highest rate of emissions (20 tonnes per person). India has the lowest rate of pollution, mainly because it has proportionately less industry. Spain and Switzerland have the fewest fumes per head among the rich countries.

Even in poor count-ries, most children now attend primary school; it is secondary-school attendance (measured here as a proportion of 12–17-year-olds) that separates countries. Among the industrial economies, Australia, Britain and Italy have the least-educated workforces. Indeed, all three have lower secondary-school enrolment rates than South Korea or Hong Kong.

People like to be healthy, as well as wealthy and wise. The Japanese get the prize for longevity, living for an average of 79 years. The average Indian lives for 60 years. Russia's life expectancy (69 years) is no higher than China's, even though its income per head is four times bigger. Yet, bizarrely, Russia (equal with Italy) has more doctors per head than any other country in our sample: it has twice as many doctors as America and three times as many as Britain.

Big cities tend to suffer more violence and crime. America has the highest murder rate among rich countries, but the streets of Brazil, Mexico, Russia and the Bahamas are even more dangerous. An American man is 13 times more likely to be murdered than his counterpart in Britain or Japan. America fares badly in the family stakes, too. It has the highest divorce rate (48% of all marriages) followed by Sweden (44%). In Italy and Spain only 8% of marriages break up.

Questions

1. Economists use GDP as a measure of the standard of living. What limitations does this concept have as a measure of the quality of life?

2. The article discusses several features which affect the quality of life. What other aspects of modern life not mentioned here would give a better indication of the quality of life than GDP?

3. Given the limitations of GDP, why do you think that it is still the most frequently used measure of living standards?

Getting Europe Back to Work

Getting Europe back to work: Unemployment is Europe's most pressing domestic problem. Unlike monetary co-ordination, governments are trying to tackle it on their own – half-heartedly

AT THE European Community's summit in June, EC leaders gave Jacques Delors, the president of the European Commission, a chance to restore his battered credibility by coming up with ideas to make EC industry more competitive and thus put some of Europe's 17m unemployed back to work. He is supposed to present his proposals at the EC's next summit in December.

Meanwhile - wondering, perhaps, just how much good this curious idea would produce - European governments are seeing what they can do on their own. The pressure to shake up national labour markets is growing for several reasons. The most important is unemployment, whose rise is pushing politicians to make radical changes. By the end of this year, the EC's average unemployment rate is likely to be over 11%, compared with 7% in America and 2.5% in Japan. The European Commission thinks the rate will not fall without growth of over 2% a year. By the end of next year, the number of unemployed people in Europe could be nearing 20m - roughly equal to the populations of Greece and Portugal combined.

As the number of jobless grows, so does disillusion with the EC's single market, which was supposed to give Europe's economy a fillip. Cutting unemployment would also help governments ease the burden on their social-security systems. At present, EC countries spend between 1% and 3% of their GDPs on unemployment benefit, youth training and other labour-market schemes. This spending is likely to grow as more companies shed jobs to cut costs. On August 24th Mercedes–Benz, a German up-market car maker, said it would lay off around 8,000 workers this year. Philips, Holland's giant electronics company, plans to axe between 10,000 and 15,000 jobs this year.

Many of those who leave the job market will find it hard to get back in: nearly half of Europe's unemployed have been out of work for a year or more, compared with just 6% of America's. With footloose European companies threatening to move more of their production abroad, politicians are beginning to pay more than lip-service to labour-market reform. Even when business was booming in the 1980s,

unemployment in most European countries was uncomfortably high.

Employment has soared in America since 1965; in Europe, it has grown by only a tenth. One reason was that real wages rose faster in the EC than in America or Japan during the 1980s. But Europe's rigid labour laws made matters worse, by delaying job cuts and making employers think three times before hiring new staff. The result: more unemployment, not less.

America's hire-and-fire labour practices are still anathema to many EC governments. But they are beginning to recognise the need to stop feather-bedding workers. From Madrid to Milan, policymakers are concentrating on the following areas of reform:

Wages

To keep wage increases down, the Spanish, Italian and German governments have all sought tripartite deals involving employers, trade unions and government. For example, German unions have accepted pay restraint as part of the so-called 'solidarity pact', a deal to spread the costs of unification.

Expect debate about - if

not changes to – laws governing national minimum wages. At present, seven EC countries including France, Belgium and Spain have such legislation, which can price young workers out of jobs. Holland's Christian Democrat party recently proposed scrapping the minimum wage there, but its Socialist partners in the ruling coalition are likely to oppose this. Fred Lempers, of the Netherlands Christian Federation of Employers, says that Dutch companies are hoping that the minimum, currently 2,163 guilders (£760) a month, will at least be halved.

Unemployment and social benefits

These are particularly generous in Germany, the home of Europe's most coddled workers. But for how much longer? On August 11th, Theo Waigel, Germany's finance minister, said he wanted cuts in some benefits, including unemployment pay and social-security hand-outs. As well as scrapping maternity pay and reducing some child-care allowances, Mr Waigel's proposals, which have not yet been approved by parliament, would abolish special payments to building workers temporarily laid off because of bad weather. The French government is trying to lighten the burden of social charges on employers. In his recently unveiled five-year plan, Michel Giraud, the labour minister, said that the government would progressively start paying the social-security costs now borne by employers for the families of workers earning up to 1.5 times the minimum wage. On one estimate, this could save companies up to FFr8 billion (£1 billion) this year. Companies will also be freed for a limited period from paying social-security taxes for newly hired staff.

Labour flexibility

As well as making it cheaper to hire workers, some governments are trying to make it easier to fire them too. In Spain, where labour laws are particularly tough, companies like to hire staff on temporary contracts because full-time employees are so hard to get rid of. More than a third of Spanish workers are employed on this basis. The government hopes that by loosening laws and offering financial incentives, it can persuade employers to hire more full-timers. French companies too find inflexible labour laws prevent them adjusting working patterns to changes in demand. The government wants to allow this. Its new labour measures include one lifting the 39-hour restriction on the working week, replacing it with an annualized equivalent. This means that in some weeks employees can be asked to work up to 48 hours, providing that they can take more time off when business is less brisk.

What can Mr Delors do to help speed these reforms? Not much. Hiring and firing rules remain the responsibility of national governments, as do those affecting social-security costs and other payroll taxes. The EC's main area of action, as set out in the Social Charter (accepted by all EC countries except Britain), concerns working conditions and health and safety rules. Nevertheless, Mr Delors has called for more training, and for more and better-quality employment agencies. He is also plotting heavy investment in pan-European infrastructure projects. These may help shorten the dole queues for a time; but they are mere palliatives unless EC governments get serious about radical labour-market reforms.

The Essence of the Story

- Unemployment is forcing politicians to make radical choices.

- Unemployment is higher in Europe than in the United States and half of Europe's unemployed have been out of work for a year or more compared to 6 per cent in the United States.

- One reason for high unemployment in Europe is that real wages have risen.

- Rigid labour laws make matters worse.

- Policy makers are seeking to keep down wages, scrap minimum wages, cut unemployment pay and make it easier to fire workers.

- Since hiring and firing rules are the responsibility of national governments, there is little that the European Union can do to reduce unemployment.

Background and Analysis

The underlying theoretical approach here is typical of The Economist – great emphasis on market forces. Labour is analysed very much as any other market; if supply exceeds demand,

the solution is to cut the price – in this case the wage.

Diagrammatically, the article assumes that wages are at W_1 when the equilibrium wage would be W_2. The result is unemployment of A-B. The solution is to cut wages to W_2.

Critics of this approach would argue that the labour market is different from other markets; for example labour is less mobile than consumer goods, so that the market may never reach equilibrium.

Keynesian economists would argue that the article focuses exclusively on supply side aspects and ignores the importance of aggregate demand in determining demand for labour.

Critics would also point out that the American approach leads to great poverty, homelessness and crime.

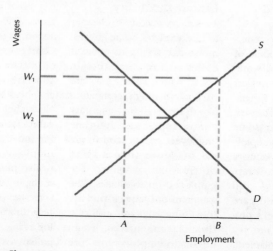

Figure 19.1

Questions

1. Explain why the author suggests that a rise in real wages will lead to a rise in unemployment.

2. Explain what is meant by a minimum wage and summarize the arguments for and against its introduction in the United Kingdom.

3. What do you think is meant by 'labour flexibility'? Show why the author thinks that

it will reduce unemployment. What additional factors would Keynesian economists suggest to reduce unemployment?

4. What factors other than those mentioned in the article could have been responsible for low unemployment in the United States?

Nothing for Everyone

Jacques Delors' ideas to solve Europe's unemployment

'IF IT were easy to obtain full employment again, it wouldn't be necessary for the Commission and the Council to discuss it. There is no single miracle cure.'

Forgive Jacques Delors, president of the European Commission, for stating the obvious. He had just spent a wearying session failing to persuade Europe's finance ministers (the Council) to adopt his remedy for unemployment in the European Union (formerly the Community). He will try again. No one doubts the gravity of the problem. At least 17m, or over 11% of the labour force, are out of work. But few politicians are keen to swallow Mr Delors' medicine.

Strip away the heroic assumptions (that his scheme will push investment from 19% of GDP to 23–24% and that at least 15m new jobs will be created, 'thereby halving the current rate of unemployment by the year 2000'). Even then, the finance ministers' preview of his 'white paper on growth, competitiveness and employment' contains proposals to annoy virtually everyone.

Take Mr Delors' enthusiasm for work-sharing. The idea has its fans. Several companies in France, Germany and Italy have, or are thinking about, four-day weeks. But if working fewer hours cured unemployment, why is joblessness higher in Europe than in America and Japan, where the working week is longer? Luxembourg's minister, Jean-Claude Junker, described the idea as 'defeatist'; Britain's Kenneth Clarke called it 'folly'. Add to that the criticism from Gert Haller, a state secretary at Germany's finance ministry, that the Commission's proposals for a big cut in interest rates amount to 'exchange-rate dumping' and Mr Delors might well feel bruised.

If so, he does not show it. 'I don't understand the obsession of Clarke that there should always be a clear victor. Do we have to install a cricket pitch at our meetings?' he asks. One reason for his resilience may be that his critics have even less support than he has. Britain's espousal of labour-market deregulation and less social featherbedding is caricatured across the Channel as a return to sweat-shops. The day after the finance ministers met, Britain's employment secretary, David Hunt, was pointedly alone in opposing a directive to limit the working week to 48 hours, and in blocking a Commission proposal to give three months' parental leave to both Ma and Pa.

All this leaves the Union in a familiar deadlock of incompatible philosophies: free-marketeering in Britain; 'social partnership' between workers and employers from Germany to Italy; grand designs in France – witness President Mitterrand's recent proposal for a 100 billion ecu bond to finance trans-European road, rail and telecoms networks.

Mr Delors likes this sort of thing. The preview of his white paper waxes enthusiastic – and expensive – on trans-European infrastructure and increased spending for research and technology development. On infrastructural links between the Union and the new markets of ex-communist Eastern Europe, Mr Delors says: 'I consider reasonable a programme varying between 20 billion and 30 billion ecus a year.' Big money. Unless private investors share the burden (their lack of enthusiasm for the Channel tunnel serves as a salutory warning), the weight would have to be borne by taxpayers at a time when the Maastricht treaty has decreed a reduction in government spending. Mr Delors's hopes for a Rooseveltian New Deal may be in vain.

So is it gloom all along Europe's lengthening dole queues? Not necessarily. In the second half of the 1980s, when Europe was preparing for a single market in goods, capital, services and people, some 9m new jobs were created. More trade could yet create millions of new jobs, and Mr Delors, the most imaginative president in the Commission's 35 years, could end his term with honour.

Questions

1. What do you think is meant by 'free marketeering' and 'social partnership'? Summarize and then assess the arguments of supporters of these ideas.

2. How can trade create jobs?

3. The idea of spending billions of ecu on infrastructure is linked to the ideas of Keynes. Critically summarize these ideas.

Doleful

Europe does indeed provide America with useful lessons about unemployment – about the policies to be avoided, not adopted

IF THE jobs of labour ministers and labour economists were tied to the success of their policies, most of them would be joining the 35m people – 8.5% of the workforce – in the rich world's still-lengthening unemployment queues. Instead, many of them from around the world will be jet-setting to America next month for an unemployment summit hosted by Bill Clinton.

They do have plenty to talk about: the OECD expects rich-world unemployment to hit 36m early next year (including a frightening 12.2% of the European Community workforce) before it begins to fall. But early hints of the American agenda suggest that the summiteers will be energetically seeking to develop further the methods that have helped cause the problem in the first place.

Why has unemployment in the OECD soared? Some economists blame what they think has been an over-zealous fight against inflation. They call upon governments to spur output and create jobs by cutting interest rates and easing fiscal policies. But although Europe's high interest rates have clearly prolonged its recession, only part of the recent rise in unemployment can be blamed on the downturn.

After all, unemployment in the EC has averaged 10%, and never once dipped below 8%, for the past ten years. So another school of thought pins the blame on competition – 'unfair' competition, you understand – from developing countries. On this view, the obvious solution is to preserve jobs by raising trade barriers. In fact, no trade barrier will keep out the technological changes that are revolutionising work in the rich world; and a trade war is sure to destroy more jobs than it saves.

President Clinton and his labour secretary, Robert Reich, claim to agree that neither reckless reflation nor protectionism is the right remedy for worsening joblessness. But they are toying with a third method that would be no better. Among the ideas gaining currency in the administration are increases in the minimum wage, wider social-security benefits and measures to make it harder for firms to sack workers. America, it seems, wants to be more like Europe.

That would be perverse. Unemployment in the Community averages 12% of the labour force, compared with less than 7% in America. Worse still, almost half of Europe's jobless have been on the dole for more than a year; in America the equivalent figure is only 11%. It is even more striking that, while the number of American jobs has almost doubled since 1960, EC employment has risen by a paltry 10%. So 77% of Americans of working age, but only 67% of those in the EC, now have jobs.

These figures suggest that Europe has more to learn from America than the other way around. There is a growing awareness in Europe that high unemployment is the result of over-regulated and inflexible labour markets. Europe's generous social-security benefits give the unemployed little incentive to seek work. Minimum wages, intended to protect the low-paid, instead cost young workers their jobs. France's minimum wage was increased sharply in the 1980s, to more than 50% of average earnings; America's has fallen to about 30%. It is no coincidence that a quarter of France's people under 25 years of age are unemployed, roughly twice the share in America. Employers' social-security contributions and other non-wage costs add, on average, an extra 30% to wage costs in the EC (almost 50% in Germany).

As with everything else, higher prices mean less demand – in this case, the demand of employers for workers. Firms in Europe are further discouraged from hiring by strict employment-protection rules that make it hard, if not impossible, to lay off workers once they are on the payroll.

So look not to Europe for answers. Better to ask whether the recent gloom about 'jobless growth' in America has been overdone. After all, almost 3m jobs have been created in America since early 1991. There is understandable concern about their quality. Too many, say the merchants of gloom, are part-time, temporary and badly paid. The real wages of low-skilled workers have fallen over the past decade. Yet,

in comparison with Europe, this should be seen as a sign of success – an example of a well-functioning labour market – not a failure. As manufacturing has declined, America and Europe have both faced shrinking demand for low-skilled labour. In America, the relative pay of these workers was allowed to fall, so fewer jobs were lost. European workers, by contrast, have resisted the inevitable and so priced themselves out of work.

In the long term, the way to create more well-paid jobs in both America and in Europe is through better education and training. But this takes time. In the short term,

there is no substitute for flexible wages. That is exactly why so many Europeans nowadays want to make their labour markets less rigid, rather than more. The French government is planning to cut the minimum wage for young workers and to trim company payroll taxes. Other EC countries are loosening employment-protection laws. How ironic it would be if, at the very moment when the EC begins at last to free its labour markets, America moves to restrict them. Rather than invite Europeans to a summit in America, maybe Mr Clinton should visit Europe, to see his 'cure' in action.

Questions

1. Explain how cutting interest rates and an easy fiscal policy can reduce unemployment.

2. Why does the author suggest that another trade war will destroy more jobs than it saves?

3. What does the author suggest that Europe can learn from America? What criticisms of these arguments can you make?

4. What policies would you advocate to reduce unemployment in Europe?

363 Quadrillion Per Cent Inflation

Serbia's economic nightmare

'I AM waiting to die,' said a pensioner who cannot afford to pay for the medicine needed for his heart. Tanjug, the Serbian state news agency, dutifully intones that there are no medicines because of the world's sanctions against Serbia. It has even said that sanctions had caused a famine. Strange, since Serbia's private chemists' shops are bursting with imported medicines and its markets are groaning with food.

When sanctions were introduced in May 1992, doomsayers predicted the economy would 'collapse' within three months. It buckled, but still eerily stands. The truth is that the costs of running a war and of subsidising Serb military operations outside Serbia – plus huge incompetence – have done as much as sanctions to produce today's nightmare economy.

Some Serbs have become extremely rich; most have become much poorer. In a shop in the centre of Belgrade the wealthy ponder purchases of expensive new sanctions-busting Italian kitchen units that cost 1,000 times the average annual salary. But you cannot buy milk to put in your new fridge. Dairy farmers refuse to sell their produce at prices set by government fiat. Petrol falls under the international embargo, but unlike milk and beer its price is not controlled, so it is available at private pumps. Food costs more in Belgrade than in London. The average monthly salary is worth a mere DM20 (£8).

Pensioners, as always, are hardest hit of all. In August inflation soared astronomically to 1,880%. At an annualised rate, that is 363,000,000,000,000,000%. So the government clamped on price controls, especially on food. Inflation duly subsided a bit in September but, because of the controls, shops were reluctant to sell anything. In late September the government let prices rise again, and goods began to creep back into the shops.

It is hard to believe that any attempt to bring in strict price controls, or to regulate the shortages, is going to work. There is no administration to manage it, no omnipotent political party to supervise it. Basic goods have been put on ration but the ration coupons can be bought in the marketplace. Almost two-thirds of all trade is believed to take place in this grey economy. Barter, predictably, is taking over from normal trade. A glue company sends glue to a meat factory so that it can stick its labels on its meat cans. In return the glue firm gets meat to give its workers.

Most large firms are working at about 30% of capacity. The exceptions include some companies close to the porous borders of Bulgaria and Macedonia. Much sanctions-busting is done via Albania and Greece. According to one estimate, the rump Yugoslav state somehow exported enough in the first half of 1993 to cover 80% of the cost of its imports.

Belgrade's Economics Institute was commissioned by the government to prepare a stabilisation plan. It said the only way to bring down inflation was to stop the uncontrolled printing of money. It added that price controls, and attempts to force producers to produce, would lead to empty shops. The government ignored its advice. The institute was proved right. A year ago the government hailed entrepreneurs as the people who would create a lean, efficient new Serbia when sanctions were lifted. Now they are blamed, along with the West, for Serbia's ills.

If goods are not reaching the shops, where are they? In nuclear shelters, apparently. Many businessmen have rented these places and made Aladdin's caves of them, only to have their stockpiles exposed to view by the hound-dogs of Serbia's financial police. Ordinary people, too, have been scrimping and saving for winter. 'I hope there are no power cuts,' says an economist, Jurij Bajec, 'because all of Serbia's GNP is in its freezers.'

Questions

1. Why is barter taking over from normal trade? What disadvantages does barter have in normal circumstances?

2. Summarize the effects of hyperinflation and analyse the policies that can be used to end it.

3. What are the causes of hyperinflation?

4. Explain the paradox of a famine while there is food in the shops.

The Pain of Deflation

Can too little inflation be as harmful for an economy as too much?

A GROWING number of economists fear that Japan may now face another year of stagnation. Japan's industrial production has already tumbled by more than 10% since 1991; and there could be worse to come.

One particular worry is that Japan could find itself with outright deflation – falling consumer prices – next year, which would further weaken its economy. Wholesale prices have already been falling for two years; in October they were 3.2% lower than a year earlier. That is not unusual in Japan. In 1986–87 the slump in oil prices and the rising yen caused wholesale prices to fall at an annual rate of around 10%. Falling consumer prices, however, are less common. They dipped briefly in 1987, but this mainly reflected the drop in oil prices.

The underlying inflation rate is only 1%. Furthermore, Japan's official consumer-price index (CPI) may well overstate inflation. Apart from the usual measurement problems of price indices, such as failing to take full account of improvements in the quality of goods, Japan's CPI does not yet reflect a recent shift in spending away from traditional retailers to discount stores. From next year, it will include the effect of discount shopping.

Another source of downward pressure on inflation is the lagged impact of the yen's appreciation. According to James Capel, a London securities firm, every 10% appreciation of the yen reduces the consumer-price index by 1.5% in the first year and by a further 1.5% over the following two years. James Capel is forecasting that consumer prices could be falling by 1% year-on-year by the second half of 1994.

If high inflation is bad news, then surely falling prices – or a negative inflation rate – is good news?

Only up to a point. A fall in the price of a few products, such as computers or video-cassette recorders, is certainly good news for consumers. A fall in the overall price level, however, can prove troublesome. Indeed, in some cases, such as the 1930s, deflation can be even nastier than hyperinflation.

Traditional economic theory used to stress the positive impact of falling prices – the 'real balance effect'. Falling prices, it was argued, boosted the real value of savings. Households that felt wealthier would then spend more. However, falling prices can have the opposite effect. In particular, they swell the real value of debts. Indebted consumers and firms are likely to reduce, not increase, spending. As a recent analysis by another British securities firm, SG Warburg, points out, this matters especially in an economy like Japan's, where both households and firms are overburdened with debt.

Falling consumer prices may also encourage households to defer purchases in the hope that products will soon be cheaper. The consequent drop in demand could force prices even lower. Meanwhile, Japan's wage flexibility, usually one of its strengths, could also work against economic recovery. In Western Europe, for example, where wages are sticky downwards, falling prices would deliver real wage gains and so support consumer demand. In Japan, by contrast, wages respond quickly even to reductions in prices, through smaller bonuses and reduced overtime.

Perhaps the most serious of all the consequences of falling prices is that because interest rates cannot be negative, falling prices can also lead to punishingly high real interest rates. The Bank of Japan has already cut its discount rate to 1.75% – a real rate of roughly 0.25%. If next year the 12-month rate of inflation were minus 1%, then even if the discount rate were cut to zero, real interest rates would be forced up. When consumer prices were falling by an annual average of 6.8% in America in 1930–33, real interest rates remained stuck at painfully high levels. Monetary policy became all-but-impotent as a tool to revive demand. Falling consumer prices over a sustained period could certainly prolong Japan's downturn and make for a more muted recovery.

But thankfully there is no need for a repeat of the deflationary 1930s. Although interest rates may be an ineffective weapon when prices are falling, that still leaves fiscal policy. Japan is the only big industrial country that does not have a big budget deficit. Indeed, its total budget (at all levels of government) is roughly in balance. This means that it can afford a large fiscal boost. If Japan does suffer a nasty dose of deflation, the government will have only itself to blame. It would be a bitter irony if the only industrial economy that can prudently afford a 'Keynesian' stimulus failed to deliver it.

Questions

1. Say what is meant by a price index and explain 'the usual measurement problems of price indices'.

2. Why does an appreciation in a currency lead to downward pressure on inflation?

3. Summarize the reasons given in the article why a fall in prices can be harmful.

4. Show how a 'Keynesian stimulus' can help economic recovery.

There was an Old Lady...

Independent Central banks

CENTRAL-BANK independence has become all the rage; yet the British government is stubbornly opposed to the idea. But were Britain to join a European Monetary Union, under the Maastricht treaty it would be required to make its central bank independent.

That may be far off. However, as soon as next month the cross-party House of Commons Treasury and Civil Service Select Committee is expected to come out in favour of an independent Bank of England. A new report by an independent panel, chaired by Lord Roll (president of SG Warburg and in 1968–77 a director of the Bank of England) and published by the Centre for Economic Policy Research (CEPR), does so as well. It argues that the Bank should be given full control of monetary policy and charged with the sole aim of price stability.

The economic case for an independent central bank has been well aired. Its independence delivers politicians from temptation – to slash interest rates before an election, for example. More broadly, by bolstering the credibility of a country's anti-inflationary policy, it should make implementing it easier. Countries with independent central banks have tended to have lower inflation. Nor is there an inevitable cost in slower growth.

Not all economists agree with the argument. Days before the CEPR report, Adam Posen, an economist at Harvard, won second prize in the 1993 Amex Bank Review competition with an essay arguing that the causal link between central-bank independence and low inflation is illusory. Mr Posen reckons that a central bank can impose strong anti-inflationary medicine only when there is a powerful coalition of interests in the country capable of protecting the institution. In industrial economies, he says, this role is played by the financial sector. If there seems to be a link between central-bank independence and low inflation, it is because countries whose financial sector is most opposed to inflation are also the most eager for their central banks to be independent. In other words, countries' differing tolerance of inflation may partly reflect the sorts of financial systems they have. Mr Posen reckons, for example, that countries with a universal banking system are likely to oppose inflation more strongly: lending tends to be more significant than securities in such systems, he says, and so the financial sector is more aware of the costs of inflation. And countries whose central banks do not regulate financial institutions are often keener against inflation.

Germany and Switzerland, which have historically had both the most independent central banks and the lowest inflation, have universal banking. They also divorce their central banks from bank supervision. An independent Bank of England would make no noticeable dent in inflation so long as Britain's financial system is based mainly on securities and banks are regulated by the central bank, says Mr Posen.

The author ignores, however, the recent experience of New Zealand. Like Britain, it does not have universal banking; and its central bank is responsible for bank supervision. Yet since being made independent in 1990, the Reserve Bank of New Zealand has managed to reduce inflation to 1% and, more important, to keep it there.

Mr Posen is nevertheless right to inject some political reality into the debate. In Britain, too many people see central-bank independence as a painless way to reduce inflation and interest rates. There is no easy fix that will produce low inflation without some short-run loss of output and jobs. Unless people accept this, an independent Bank of England could soon lose its charter. But Mr Posen is wrong to dismiss independence altogether. Central-bank independence would surely help fight inflation.

A more interesting question is what form independence should take in Britain. The CEPR report examines two different models: Germany's Bundesbank and the Reserve Bank of New Zealand. It rejects the German model, in which the central bank has been given complete statutory independence, with no specific target, and trusted to do its job. That may be acceptable to inflation-fearing Germans, but British voters would never put the same trust in their central bank. Greater accountability and transparency are therefore essential. The Treasury select committee is thought to be leaning towards the New Zealand model, under which the government sets a precise inflation target, for which its central bank is fully accountable to parliament. The CEPR panel also favours a precise inflation target for the Bank of England, for which it would be openly accountable through routine reviews by parliamentary select committee. If those views prevail, greater independence for the bank would actually increase, not decrease, the democratic accountability that now exists. The panel believes, however, that ministers would have too much power if the government set the inflation target, as it does in New Zealand. Allow the Bank to set the target itself, urges the report. But it accepts that the government should have the right to override the target in extreme circumstances, seeking parliamentary approval to suspend it for a temporary period. The snag is that if the government bore no responsibility for the target, politicians might feel freer to criticise or even dump it. Such an environment might not strengthen Britain's anti-inflationary credibility.

Questions

1. Explain what is meant by monetary policy and explain how it is operated in the United Kingdom.

2. Critically analyse the arguments for and against an independent central bank.

3. Why does low inflation lead to 'some short-run loss of output and jobs'?

To Fix or Float Exchange Rates?

**Europe's tattered ERM is only the latest of many attempts
to tame currency fluctuations. Was it right to try?**

THE gold standard, Bretton Woods, the snake and now Europe's exchange-rate mechanism (ERM): each attempt that governments have made to control exchange rates has come unstuck. Under the new, softer ERM, currencies are allowed to float by as much as 15% either side of their central rates. Many reckon that this is little different from floating. Even so, most Americans remain baffled that Europeans would rather have their exchange rates managed by bureaucrats than by the market. Yet despite the near-collapse of the ERM, most Europeans still favour some system to dampen currency fluctuations.

Is the ideal exchange-rate system the same for all countries, or does fixing suit some more than others? Oddly, the debate cuts across the usual economic divide. Free-market economists might be expected to oppose hindering market forces, but in fact they tend to be split between fixers and floaters. And it may not be so surprising, after all: during the heyday of laisser-faire policies in the late 19th century, when trade boomed and capital moved freely between countries, all the big economies tied their

currencies to gold. Even today, more than two-thirds of IMF members still manage their currency in some way. But this overstates the importance of fixed exchange rates in the world economy, because the 'floaters', which include big economies such as America and Japan, account for almost half of world exports.

To assess the relative virtues of floating and fixing, consider these questions. How big are the costs of currency instability? Roller-coaster exchange rates clearly cause uncertainty, which harms investment and trade, but the exact cost to an economy will vary according to how much it depends on overseas trade and investment. The bigger the share of trade in a country's output, the more heavily such uncertainties will weigh. And the more concentrated a country's trading pattern, the more sense it will make to try to stabilise relevant exchange rates. In Europe, exports account for 38% of Germany's GDP and 69% of Belgium's; and as much as 75% of Belgium's exports go to other EC countries. (France's exports are a less dramatic 23% of its GDP.) By contrast, exports account for

only 11% of America's GDP and are less concentrated. It is because Europe's economies are so integrated that currency instability matters. It is true that hedging allows firms to reduce risk, but it is hard (or costly) to insure for more than a few years ahead.

Does devaluation work? In other words, is a lower nominal exchange rate an effective way to reduce a trade deficit? For a devaluation to be successful, it must not be offset by higher wages – ie, workers must accept a real pay-cut. If, however, workers demand higher wages as compensation for the higher import prices caused by devaluation, the gain in competitiveness will be eroded. Putting this together with its low trade-exposure helps explain why America tends to favour floating exchange rates. America imports much less in relation to its output than all European countries, so higher import prices affect overall consumer prices much less. And real wages fall in America more easily than in Europe, thanks to a more mobile, less unionised labour force.

Do exchange rates overshoot? Even if devaluation is an effective way to correct trade imbalances, exchange rates may move to the wrong level and even in the wrong direction. The idea behind floating is that currencies should move automatically in line with inflation differences, making trade imbalances self-correcting. In practice, 95% of currency trades are done by investors and speculators, not by people with goods and services to sell. Floating exchange rates often overshoot for years at a time. Big swings, such as those in the dollar in the 1980s, skew the pattern of international competitive advantage, and the resulting trade deficits fuel protectionism. Periods with fixed exchange-rate systems, like the gold standard and Bretton Woods, have been times of trade liberalisation. Imagine the impact on Europe's single market of the kind of gyrations seen in the dollar's real exchange rate.

Which system provides the best rod to fight inflation? Monetary policy can target only one thing at a time: either inflation or the exchange rate. This is why strict monetarists used to argue that governments should control the money supply and allow the exchange rate to look after itself. The more rigid an exchange-rate system, the less freedom governments have to use interest rates to fight inflation. In practice, however, money-supply measures are often misleading and governments themselves cannot be trusted to keep a tight grip on the monetary reins. This is why European countries decided in the 1980s that tying their currencies tightly to the inflation-proof D-mark was the best way to beat inflation.

But such a system works well only as long as the anchor behaves itself. Just as America's inflationary policies damaged the dollar as the Bretton Woods anchor, so Germany's profligate policies have brought the ERM to its knees. The difference is that, rather than exporting inflation, the Bundesbank's iron rod has forced Germany to export deflation. On most grounds, however, it makes sense for Europeans to prefer their currencies tethered while Americans want their dollar free and – here's the rub – cheap.

America is far from a clean floater. When it wants to, its government tries to steer the dollar, as in its recent crude attempts to talk the dollar down against the yen. During the mid-1980s the G7 industrial countries flirted with exchange-rate targets. In the Louvre accord in February 1987, they agreed to try to stabilise the dollar within unpublished target zones. This collapsed because it was based only on talk and intervention. Governments failed to make the policy changes needed to stabilise currencies; America's spendthrift ways were out of step with those in Germany and Japan. Attempts to peg currencies without co-ordinating policies are bound to flounder. The near-collapse of the ERM is only the most recent proof.

Questions

1. Explain what is meant by fixed and floating exchange rates and why free-market economists might be expected to favour floating rates.

2. Why might a devaluation help to reduce a trade deficit?

3. Why can monetary policy not target both inflation and the exchange rate?

4. Summarize the arguments for and against floating exchange rates.

5. Explain why tying a currency's value to the Deutschmark can help beat inflation.

Guilty on All Counts

The world's worst protectionists

PETER SUTHERLAND, the new director-general of the GATT, has issued a blunt little pamphlet on the costs of trade protection. Its title is 'Trade, the Uruguay Round and the Consumer', but its subtitle better conveys its tone – 'The Sting: How Governments Buy Votes on Trade with the Consumer's Money'.

Really, it's that good. Seven snappy pages explain what every citizen should know about trade but governments are too craven to confess. Distilling the evidence, Mr Sutherland says that farm support (through higher prices and taxes) costs rich-country consumers $353 billion a year. In America, each consumer pays on average $360 a year; in the EC, $450; in Japan, $600.

He singles out sugar in America (its wholesale price is 23 cents a pound, nearly double the market price); rice in Japan (which costs four to five times what it should); milk in Canada (which is more than twice as dear as in America). Mr Sutherland points out that restrictions on Japanese car imports have forced British and American buyers to pay much higher prices; and that restrictions on imports of textiles and clothing cost a typical family $200–420 a year in America, $220 a year in Canada and up to $130 a year in Britain.

And because trade-policy taxes fall most heavily on goods such as basic foods and cheap clothing, they are regressive. In Canada one study showed that the tax-rate levied by barriers to imports of clothes was three times higher for poor families than for rich ones.

What, he asks in conclusion, will the Uruguay round do for the consumer? It will lower tariffs; remove many quota restrictions on imports; curb the use of disguised protection (in the form of anti-dumping and countervailing-duty procedures); reduce wasteful subsidies; cut support for agriculture and increase competition in farm trade; gradually dismantle the Multifibre Arrangement which rigs global trade in cloth and clothes; and start to eradicate trade in counterfeit (and sometimes unsafe) products. In short, it will significantly improve 'prices, choice and quality for consumer products across the board'. It is a message that needs to be hammered home.

Trade policy is a scandal, and there can be no excuse for failing to reform it. *Floreat* Sutherland.

Questions

1. Why do farm support policies and import restrictions harm consumers?

2. Explain what is meant by 'regressive' and show how restrictions on trade can be regressive.

3. Find out and comment on the results of the Uruguay Round of the GATT. (You can find this information from a CD-ROM newspaper search, or from a recent economics textbook.)

Japan's Troublesome Imports

Does Japan block imports? The question is as old as boy meets girl. But nobody believes the answer.

DOES Japan import as much as it ought to, given its size and state of development? One thing is certain: Japan does import a lot, so its markets are by no means closed. As the table on the right shows, in 1990 Japan was the world's third-largest importer, buying $235 billion-worth of goods. This was $52 billion less than it exported, which is why it had a trade surplus that other countries complain about. But its imports are what matter for judging the openness of its markets.

Those imports are clustered in a striking way. As the table below shows, Japan exports very little food, raw materials or fuels, but imports a lot of these; by contrast it imports relatively few motor vehicles or other machinery, which it exports a lot of. What that suggests is that Japan follows the principle of comparative advantage: exporting what it is good at making, and importing what it is less good at making.

Does it import enough, however? As a proportion of GDP, both Japan and America score low compared with West European countries: 8% and 10% respectively, compared with 23% in western

World's top ten importers 1990

	Value dollars bn	Share of world imports, %	Imports per head, dollars
United States	517	14.3	2,050
Germany[1]	356	9.9	4,460
Japan	235	6.5	1,900
France	234	6.5	4,150
Britain	223	6.2	3,890
Italy	182	5.0	3,160
Holland	126	3.5	8,460
Canada	124	3.4	4,660
USSR	121	3.3	4,180
Belgium-Lux	120	3.3	11,540

Sources: GATT; OECD [1]Unified Germany

Japan's trade by category, 1990

	Exports dollars bn	Imports dollars bn
Foodstuffs	1.6	31.6
Raw materials	1.9	28.5
Fuels	1.3	56.7
Chemical products	15.9	16.0
Motor vehicles	51.0	6.4
Other machinery & transport equipment	150.3	31.5
Other manufactures	60.3	57.9
Miscellaneous	4.6	6.2

Sources: OECD; Japanese Ministry of Finance

Germany. Ranked by imports per head of population, Japan also comes out low: at $1,900 it has less than half the imports per head of Germany or France. But it is only a sliver behind America's $2,050. Which should Japan be compared with? Critics think it should be like Germany, since it has no natural resources and is not a large, continental economy like America; others think its geographical isolation from other rich countries, plus a GDP that is second only to America's in size, makes that country a more relevant comparison.

In any case, Japan's $235 billion total does not, of itself, refute the charge that Japan blocks some imports: perhaps planners merely choose to import this much, while markets would import more. In other words, do price signals operate in Japan? There was a handy experiment in 1985–90, when exchange rates between the yen, dollar and D-mark swung sharply. It took Japan's trade flows almost two years to respond to this shift in the terms of trade, but then they did, spectacularly. In 1985–90 imports rose by 84% in dollar terms; during that period, the yen had risen by 65% against the dollar and 26% in trade-weighted terms.

This could simply mean that the blockages were constant, and market forces swirled around them, rather like tidal water around rocks in a bay. So are tariff and non-tariff barriers high? Japan's average tariff on industrial products is 2.6%, compared with 3% in America and 2.9% in the EC. Non-tariff barriers, such as quotas, licences and voluntary export restraints grew to replace tariffs in many countries in the 1980s, but a World Bank study shows that the extent of such barriers in Japan is similar to that in America – which means both

have risen. Japan uses more non-tariff barriers to protect agriculture than America, but America protects more of its manufacturers this way. Agriculture is the area in which Japan is most guilty of formal protection: its farm support is about 50% higher than the OECD average. An OECD study reckoned that in 1988 this put a burden on Japanese taxpayers and consumers of $90 billion a year, or 3.2% of GDP.

Arguments about Japan's propensity to import have moved on from these formal barriers to informal ones such as culture, industrial structure and bureaucratic discretion. Culture and official meddling cannot be measured; anecdote suggests they do affect imports. But economists are supposed to be above anecdote. So recent attention has dwelt on industrial structure: do Japan's close-knit industrial groups restrain imports?

The best study on this issue[1], by Robert Lawrence of the Brookings Institution in Washington, DC, concludes that these groups do repel imports, but is hard-pressed

to say by how much. One of the problems is definition: what is a group? The same method of classification used by Mr Lawrence, taken from Dodwell Marketing Consultants, has at different times found there to be 17 keiretsu or 47 – and it is not because the habit has spread.

The other difficulty lies in drawing a conclusion: if keiretsu do repel imports, is that a cause for grievance? To those who think all import repulsion is bad, the answer will seem obvious. But, as Gary Saxonhouse of the University of Michigan points out in a comment attached to Mr Lawrence's article, his definition of a keiretsu – a group which prefers to buy from within itself rather than outside – is self-condemning. Mr Saxonhouse reckons that in many cases keiretsu firms buy from fellow group members because it is commercially advantageous – in other words, it follows comparative advantage. Nothing unfair about that.

1 'Efficient or exclusions? The Import Behaviour of Japanese Corporate Groups.' Brookings Papers, 1991 volume 1.

Questions

1. Explain what is meant by 'comparative advantage'. What comparative advantage do you think Japan has compared to other countries?

2. What informal barriers can reduce imports?

Do you think that anything can be done to reduce these barriers?

3. Use the table to find which three countries have most imports per head. Can you think of any reason to explain this?

A Guide to GATT

THE trade talks known as the Uruguay round are the eighth in the history of the General Agreement on Tariffs and Trade. Only 23 countries took part in the first, which were held in Geneva in 1947 and finished within the year. By contrast, the current round has 116 participants and has lasted more than seven years. Each round builds on the work of those that came before it. In the early days the main job was cutting tariffs, and then cutting them again. The average tariff has fallen from almost 40% when the GATT was founded to 4.7% now – and will be as little as 3% if the Uruguay round succeeds.

GATT has gradually moved into other areas too. The Kennedy round introduced rules against dumping exports. The Tokyo round made it harder for countries to manipulate technical standards, import licences and customs regulations in order to keep imports out. Some countries also signed agreements on government procurement, civil aircraft, and beef and dairy products.

If there is a single principle at the heart of GATT, it is that discrimination poisons trade. Every country in GATT opens its markets equally to every other. In practice, once a country and its largest trading partners have agreed to cut a tariff, usually in exchange for an equivalent cut elsewhere, the cut is automatically extended to every other country (the 'most-favoured-nation' principle). The new tariff cannot later be raised except by negotiations in which all other countries are compensated.

Other, murkier forms of protection are banned. Small countries enjoy better access to bigger countries' markets through GATT than they could ever have negotiated by themselves. Trade tension is defused because protectionist lobbies have less opportunity to manipulate bilateral trade (though America's tortured relationship with Japan shows that this does not always happen). And GATT holds that countries should treat foreign businessmen as they do locals, banning bogus rules designed to circumvent this principle of 'national treatment'.

There are few permitted exceptions to discrimination, but they are increasingly prominent. Regional trading areas are allowed as long as they cover most trade and do not raise trade barriers to outsiders. Countries can discriminate in favour of developing countries; and they can increase protection temporarily in emergencies – when an industry is in dire trouble, or when a country suffers from an unmanageable current-account deficit.

The Uruguay round's seven predecessors have had a profound effect on the world economy. Between 1950 and 1975 the volume of world trade expanded five-fold and the world economy more than doubled in size. But since growth in trade and output slowed in the 1970s, GATT's rules have been undermined.

The Uruguay round seeks to put this right in four ways: further cuts in tariffs; reforming GATT as an institution; eliminating damaging exceptions to GATT's universal coverage of goods; and bringing in new items to make GATT more relevant. Nothing in the Uruguay round is agreed on until all countries initial the entire package. But much has been settled provisionally over the past seven years. The details are contained in the 'draft final act', 450 pages long and comprising 28 separate agreements.

The act's main provisions would aim to:

* Write for the first time a set of rules to cover trade in services. A framework would exist for the liberalisation, not only of the $900 billion-worth of services that cross borders, but also the $3 trillion-worth of services that are provided domestically around the world – insurance, for example. The modest progress sought in this round would supply a platform for more liberalisation in future rounds.

* Protect all kinds of intellectual property, including patents, copyright and trademarks. That would be good for developed countries, which can collect higher royalties; but some of the developing countries might lose.

* Phase out over ten years the bilateral quotas which make up the multifibre arrangement for textiles and clothing. Tariffs will be cut. Developing countries should benefit.

* Forge a comprehensive agreement in GATT's biggest exception, farm trade. The details are unresolved, but the principles are clear: replace quotas with tariffs; and cut subsidies, especially export subsidies.

* Cut tariffs by at least a third. Tariffs imposed by the big economies on some important items will be eliminated altogether. Special attention has been given to a few very high tariffs; and to helping developing countries by cutting tariffs on tropical products.

* Try to reform (successfully) the rules against subsidies. Try to curb (minimally) the misuse of rules on dumping. Try to prevent (hopelessly) the use of voluntary export restraints – a sort of import quota which is operated by an exporter under pressure from an importing country.

* Tidy up rules on shipment, including inspection, customs, import licensing, technical standards and rules of origin. Phase out trade-related investment measures, such as the requirement that foreign investors buy supplies locally.

* Build on earlier agreements in government procurement and civil aircraft.

* Speed up the arbitration of disputes between GATT members. Countries will also find it harder to dissent from judgments.

* Clarify a raft of GATT rules. Transform GATT from a provisional agreement (it was never ratified by America) into a full institution called the Multilateral Trade Organisation.

COPYRIGHT © THE ECONOMIST NEWSPAPER LIMITED, LONDON (DECEMBER 1993)

Questions

1. Explain what is meant by 'intellectual property', 'quotas', 'dumping', and 'voluntary export restraints'.

2. Draw a diagram to show the effects of a tariff. What benefits accrue from the reduction of tariffs?

3. Summarize the main points of the Uruguay round of GATT. What effects do you think this agreement will have on world trade?

4. Why should GATT want to replace quotas by tariffs?

Part G: Comparative Economics

Japan in a Bind
The trouble with the Japanese economy

SOUND everyday management is the Japanese government's strength, but when it comes to bold reform the politicians tend to duck. So it is that, despite much talk of changing the electoral system and the laws on financing political parties, Japan has so far seen no Italianate reaction to corruption scandals. Equally serious, recession has not inspired Japan's government to economic reform.

This failure may be gnawing at the roots of Japan's post-war success. Japan's real GDP shrank 0.1% in the fourth quarter of last year and few expect much of a recovery before the end of this year. The government's response has been to pump demand into the economy. Two special spending programmes, worth Y 23.9 trillion ($214 billion), announced in the past year, have helped ward off full-blown recession, and the government has propped up the stockmarket by shovelling post-office savings money into it.

Satisfied with attending to the symptoms of the economy's problems, the government has not applied itself to tackling some of their causes. Japan protects and regulates parts of the economy where imports and other sorts of competition ought to flourish. In the food industry, the rice grown by Japan's protected farmers costs several times as much as it does abroad. In service industries, regulation and protection have allowed Japanese companies to be around half as productive as America's. In the construction industry, red tape, along with the endemic bribery so sharply illustrated by the recent Sagawa Kyubin scandal, means that foreigners get virtually no contracts: last year Americans got 0.02% of them. And restrictive regulations, which keep Tokyo buildings low and living spaces small, stifle one of the economy's biggest potential areas for consumption and imports.

Such inefficiencies clash painfully with hyper-efficient manufacturing. Japan's car makers and machine makers are among the best in the world – hence the country's much resented $10 billion-a-month trade surplus. This surplus pushes up the yen, which ought to boost imports. Yet imports stay low, partly because foreign firms do not always try hard enough to crack Japan, but partly because of over-regulation.

Sometimes the impact of regulations on imports is straightforward: foreign rice is all but banned. Sometimes red tape cuts the advantage that efficient foreigners should have; this is the plight of financial and legal firms. The effect of building regulation is still more roundabout. By making it hard to put up the tall blocks of flats of the sort that span the skylines of most capitals, the government condemns Tokyo to low-rise, cramped housing. That deprives Japanese of the space that, in other rich countries, would be used to accommodate the domestic fantasies whose purchase occupies the weekends and disposes of the earnings of workers.

With little scope for investing in new kitchens or spending on three-piece suites, the Japanese put their money in the bank. So savings rates stay high, and consumption, including the consumption of imported goods, stays low. Such distortions lead to a persistent trade surplus and a persistently rising yen. This is bad news not merely for Japan's relations with America but also for ordinary Japanese. The higher the yen rises, the harder the country's exporters must strain to stay competitive. Japan's big firms are not given to sacking workers publicly. Beneath the surface, however, restructuring goes on. The number of jobs in the economy is still rising slightly, but permanent jobs are scarcer: white-collar permanent employment fell by 2.9% in the year to March, blue-collar by 1.8%, according to Jesper Koll, of SG Warburg.

Those who keep their jobs are also affected. Overtime pay is down 15% from its peak two years ago; summer bonuses are expected to fall 1.6% this year, the largest drop on record. Bankruptcies, especially among the big firms' small suppliers, are at a record. In the year to March they resulted in job losses of more than 110,000. Ironically, this burden is falling upon Japan's efficient export industries as much as on inefficient, over-regulated ones. Worse, the high yen is forcing

exporters to move to cheaper sites in Asia. Japan risks losing the industries it is good at, and being lumbered with the rest.

The Japanese have the second-highest average incomes in the world. This puzzles them: they ask why, if they are so rich, life is not easier. Part of the reason is that their earnings are dissipated by prices kept high by import controls. Spotted in a Tokyo supermarket: six peaches for Y 4,200 ($38). Other regulations do their bit; Tokyo residents have to commute huge distances because building restrictions limit the living space available in the capital. The frustration of unrewarded effort reinforces other creeping changes. Japan's tradition of lifetime employment is based on the fast growth of the 1960s and 1970s. In those days Japan's firms borrowed technology from abroad, then trained their workers to apply it. To make the training

pay off, firms did their best to keep employees; at the same time, the prospect of training gave employees an incentive to stay with their firms. Now that Japan has caught up technologically, growth is inevitably slower. The reason for companies' single-minded loyalty to their workers is fading, as is the reason for workers' loyalty to their firms.

This adds up to a threat to the source of Japan's post-war strength. Left-wing and right-wing, labour and management have never wavered from the pursuit of economic growth. Families have not questioned the breadwinner's devotion to the firm. Now different priorities are emerging. The government's current five-year plan declares that Japan must become a 'life-style superpower'. Businessmen may hope to ignore such sloganising. But if Japan's workers lose their devotion to their jobs, the bosses will have to pay attention.

Questions

1. Explain how a government can pump demand into an economy and show the results of such an operation.

2. Why does a trade surplus push up the price of a currency? Why would you expect this to boost imports?

3. Outline the reasons given in the article for the low level of imports into Japan. What are the consequences of this (a) for firms, and (b) for workers?

Not Working

Unemployment rises in Russia

BETWEEN 1929 and 1933, America's GDP shrank by 30% and over 8m Americans lost their jobs. Russia's great depression has been worse: over the past three years, its GDP is estimated to have fallen by 38%. Yet in October, say the official figures, a mere 968,000 Russians (1.3% of the workforce) were out of work. 'No economy in history has had a decline in output as sharp as Russia has experienced, without mass unemployment,' says Guy Standing, the head of the International Labour Organisation's East European team.

What is going on? The official figures are rubbish. They record the number of people who have registered with one of the 2,500 employment exchanges run by the Federal Employment Service. In Russia, being unemployed is a disgrace; until the introduction of the Employment Act of 1991, it was a crime. Those who register as unemployed face a Kafkaesque bureaucracy. Collecting the necessary documents can take months, and is often impossible for those who are working away from home and do not have a residence permit valid for their place of work – just the people who are usually the first to be sacked.

There are few incentives to register. Of those who do,

not all get unemployment benefits: anyone who received severance pay, or was dismissed for misconduct, is automatically denied help. The benefits are pathetic. Fedor Prokopov, the head of the Federal Employment Service, calculates that the government paid 18 billion roubles in unemployment benefits in the first eight months of this year. This means that each person out of work received the equivalent of roughly $3 a month.

The official statistics do, however, reflect a worrying failure of Russia's reforms. Few formerly state-owned enterprises have changed their behaviour (or their management) after privatisation, which usually leaves the workers and managers with more than half their company's shares. In many companies, a pact has been struck: the director promises not to sack anyone; in return the workers agree to use their shares to support the management. The loose monetary policy pursued by Russia's central bank has prolonged this make-believe world.

The more hopeless firms, many of them in Russia's rustbelt in the southern Urals and western Siberia, cannot deny the new reality much longer. Mr Prokopov estimates that they have already had to put 3.7m workers on

involuntary and unpaid leave, or to give them only part-time work. These people are unemployed in everything but name. If reform-minded candidates do well in the parliamentary election on December 12th, and if they then do what needs to be done to the economy, unemployment will rise sharply. It could reach 10m – 14% of the workforce, more than in any other big European country except Spain – by the end of 1994, predicts Boris Fedorov, the finance minister.

This shift from hidden to open unemployment will bring a howl of protest against economic reform. There are few signs that the supporters of reform are prepared to deal with it. Over the past five years, they have heard too many warnings that unemployment was about to explode; and, so far, it has not. Some reformists think it won't this time either. Others, the more ideological ones, hope it will: this would prove that reform is at last changing the way enterprises behave, and a higher level of unemployment would make it easier to control inflation.

Then there are the political calculations. If unemployment does shoot upwards, it will be safely after the election. And the threat from the unions is slight. They have been emasculated since the government stopped channelling social-security payments through them in October and switched to direct payments. The government thinks that only the coal-mining and defence-industry unions can still organise sustained strikes, and it is confident it could defeat them. The decline in output has led to the build-up of large coal stocks; and the drop in defence production is no longer seen as a threat to national security.

The reformers, however, have not really explained to the voters that Russia's choice is not between continued low unemployment and 10m unemployed; it is between 10m and the much bigger number who would be thrown out of work by the economic chaos that would follow an attempt to reverse reform, or even slow it down. If reform goes on, Russia's industry will waste fewer resources, inflation will fall, exports will rise, and new jobs will be created. That will make a lot of people better off – and help to offset the misery of those who are going to lose their jobs whatever happens.

Questions

1. Use the material in the article to discuss the difficulties of moving from a command to a market economy.

2. Explain what is meant by 'hidden unemployment' and why the official figures for unemployment in Russia are inaccurate. Are they accurate in your country?

3. Find out what economic reforms have taken place in Russia (for example from a CD-ROM literature search, or from a recent economics textbook). Comment on your results.

China Speeds on to Market

New market reforms

A DOCUMENT of 16,000 words called 'Decision on issues concerning the establishment of a socialist market economic structure', produced by a body called the third plenary session of the 14th Central Committee of the Communist Party of China, sounds like a sure sign of boredom ahead. But it was a similarly stupefying title, issued by an earlier session of these five-yearly meetings, that launched Deng Xiaoping's economic reforms 15 years ago. It is too early to tell whether the latest such meeting, held in Beijing between November 11th and 14th, will have such revolutionary consequences. Yet it is already clear that, despite its current worries, China's government is determined to push ahead with further reforms to create a market economy in all but name in the next few years.

Experts wading through the document's swampy prose are disappointed that this goal was not set forth with the crispness many had hoped for. They believe they see signs of a continuing battle between out-and-out free marketeers and those still fond of bits of central planning. And they also detect a power struggle over who will be running the country after the 89-year-old Mr Deng dies.

Even so, the party has left no doubt about which way it is heading. The government is to retain majority ownership of only the bigger state-owned enterprises. Even with these the aim is to 'corporatise' them, meaning to give them proper boards of directors and, unless the government is the sole owner, a joint-stock structure. Smaller state-owned firms are candidates for privatisation. Market pricing is to be extended from goods markets (where 90% of prices are now set by supply and demand) to labour, property and financial markets. The government is to start asserting control through macroeconomic instruments instead of administrative orders. The commercial banks are to be relieved of making 'policy' loans – those will become the domain of three economic-development banks – and will then have to make their own way without government help. Interest rates are to be set by the market. The central bank is to become a real central bank, instead of the government's cashier and a dabbler on its own behalf in the lending market.

A social-security system – mainly pensions, health care and unemployment – is to be set up, paid for by taxes on wages. Private insurance schemes will be allowed to supplement this. The bright young economists who have helped design the plan say that housing reform, with rents being raised closer to market levels and a market in housing slowly introduced, will also be brought in next year.

Oh, and one other thing: the Communist Party will retain its monopoly of political power. None of this will be easy. The Central Committee meeting came at a scary, though exhilarating, time for the Chinese economy – which may account for the murkiness of the document. China's reformers know what they want in the long term, but right now nobody understands for sure what is going on in the economy. China's economy grew by 13% in real terms last year and will probably grow even faster this year. Foreign investors are more enthusiastic about China than about any other emerging market. Share prices in Hong Kong have rocketed because so many foreign portfolio investors want a piece of the action in China. An amazing $83 billion-worth of foreign direct investment in China was contracted for in the first nine months of this year and $15 billion-worth actually invested, compared with $8 billion–10 billion (depending on whose figures you use) in the whole of last year. Foreign sellers are just as eager. On November 16th Helmut Kohl, Germany's chancellor, was in Beijing when 20 contracts, worth $2.8 billion, were signed for German firms to supply Chinese buyers.

China's growth has put immense inflationary strains on the economy. In July Zhu Rongji, a Deng protege who is China's economic supremo, introduced a credit squeeze intended to crush speculation in property, foreign exchange and shares. It was also intended to reassert the central government's authority over China's increasingly cocky provinces. The credit squeeze has had mixed results. Speculators have indeed been trounced in many markets. Mr Zhu has retrieved at most 60% of the speculative interbank loans that he had said at the outset he wanted to. But distress sales of property are common, foreign-exchange speculation has been stamped out and share-dealing has been brought to heel.

One macroeconomic signal is worrying: the trade deficit will probably hit $9 billion–10 billion this year, down from a surplus of $4 billion in 1992, and foreign-exchange reserves are falling. On the other hand, the currency has been stable after an early-summer plunge, and the rates of increase in fixed-asset investment and urban consumer prices have gone down.

Most significant of all, the rate of increase in the broad measure of money supply fell from 26% in June to 22% in September. All this seems to have prompted the government to declare victory in its all-of-four-months-old fight against inflation. Yet if policy is about to be relaxed, the real reason will be the government's precarious fiscal position. The official budget deficit is a tolerable 4% or so of GDP, but the true figure is at least twice that because of the deficits of the loss-making state enterprises. They, not the booming consumer-goods firms in the private part of the economy (and the still-contented consumers the private and foreign companies are supplying), are the ones that have suffered most from the recent credit squeeze. As many as a third of China's state-owned firms may be idle at present, their workers receiving minimal basic wages but sitting at home (or more likely working in private firms on the side).

The fiercest squabbles in the Central Committee document were over proposals to overhaul China's medieval tax – or rather tax-farming – system. The centre, whose tax take as a share of GDP has been halved in the past 15 years, wants to wrest more of the total take from the provinces by introducing modernish income and VAT-like taxes. If, over the next few months, China's government rescues its fiscal position through tax reform and a surreptitious liquidation of state companies, a sustainable boom of 10% real GDP growth a year for the rest of the century can be expected.

Questions

1. What are the main features of a market economy? How does it differ from a command economy? In which category would you place the Chinese economy?

2. Describe and comment on the changes taking place in the Chinese economy.

3. Why should economic growth lead to inflationary pressures?

4. Explain what is meant by a 'broad measure of money supply' and say why the author thinks that a fall in this would be desirable.

5. What is a credit squeeze? What are its effects?

Trouble on the Farm

**Agriculture in Eastern Europe and the former
Soviet Union was supposed to be in the vanguard of a
new market economy – instead it is struggling**

As THIS summer's harvest gets under way, farmers in the former communist countries are cursing. Agriculture was supposed to flourish under the fertiliser of capitalism. Look, the experts said, at China, where agrarian reform in the late 1970s conjured up an economic miracle. Look at the scope in Eastern Europe for preventing waste, improving yields and harnessing the secrets of western husbandry.

Yet the fall in output throughout Eastern Europe and the former Soviet Union has been brutal. In most countries farm output fell in 1992 by at least 10% – faster than output in the economy as a whole for the first time in recent history – largely because of a severe drought. Russia, which still has the biggest farming industry in the region, escaped: it produced 107m tonnes of grain last year, an above-average harvest compared with the past five years. This year – thanks to good weather rather than better farming –the harvest could reach as much as 125m tonnes.

If the region's problems were purely meteorological, they would be easier to solve. Instead agricultural reform has brought all sorts of institutional friction into the open. In Eastern Europe farming matters – it accounts for 20% of output and 18% of employment in Hungary. It is thus able not only to hold back the entire economy, but also to discredit the process of market-driven reform. Now Eastern Europe's despondent farmers are looking westwards and asking why, if efficient capitalist agriculture needs subsidies, they should not be protected too.

The frustration on Eastern Europe's farms is tied to the slow emergence of private ownership. A full western-style structure, dominated by family-run holdings, may never emerge from the collective farms of today. However, private ownership – even if it is co-operative – is essential for two reasons: first to create incentives for state-farm labourers, who currently toil in enormous unmotivated workforces; and second to create a capital base upon which a new agricultural industry can be built.

Capital mattered less in China where farming is labour-intensive and farmers did not need cash to buy 'inputs', such as machinery and fuel (much of the fertiliser came from the farmers themselves). Even without plentiful capital, they could rapidly respond to changing incentives. Farming in Eastern Europe, however, is capital intensive, relying on purchased inputs, such as tractors, petrol and chemicals. Only if farmers can borrow against private land can they raise enough money to set themselves up.

Aware of this, all the countries in the region have schemes of one sort or another to get land into private hands. Progress has been slow – frustrated often by both managers and labourers. Many farm managers do not want to lose their privileges, or their most enterprising staff, to the private sector. Workers are understandably reluctant to take on the full range of general farming chores, many of which are unfamiliar. In Russia, the state farm provides education, health care and a social life as well as employment. Throughout the region, the legal procedures to establish a land claim are fiendishly complicated. In the former Czechoslovakia only 180,000 out of 3.5m people eligible had applied for land by the beginning of the year. Private farms account for barely a twentieth of output in both Slovakia and the Czech Republic. All the collective farms in Hungary have been privatised, but many cannot be broken up because of legal conflicts about the ownership of land. Similarly, in

Bulgaria the bureaucracy is bogged down by more than 1.7 million conflicting claims.

Russia now has 260,000 private farmers, each with, on average, 38 hectares of land. Viktor Khlystan, the agriculture minister, optimistically predicts that by 1995 there will be 650,000 private farms with 75 hectares each. These are still tiny compared with the 25,000 remaining state and collective farms, which cultivate as much as 15,000 hectares each. In December 1991 Boris Yeltsin gave these farms six months to turn themselves into joint-stock companies, but few have changed their behaviour. At the Olginski state farm near Samara, the directors admit they have spent most of the time since the farm became a joint-stock company in late 1992 squabbling about strategy. One tractor mechanic, a workers' representative on the board, speaks for many of his colleagues: 'Who wants to be a private farmer? It's too much work.'

Worryingly, many of those who have bought land have fared poorly. In Russia they have often been given scattered plots of poor-quality land. Gale Johnson, an economist from Chicago who helped to prepare a study on Russian farming for the World Bank, argues that input industries have been slow to start making machinery small enough for private farms, and many refuse to supply them directly with chemicals. Thus smaller farms have had to buy their supplies from resentful state farms. Farmers in all the former communist countries have been trapped between the 'price scissors' of increasing costs and decreasing revenues.

Across Eastern Europe, inefficient suppliers have been jacking up prices for all manner of inputs as price controls are removed and inflation races away. However, food prices, many of which are still regulated, have risen less quickly. Not only are governments eager to keep the urban population sweet, by restricting food-price inflation, but the profit that does exist is often taken by monopolistic food processors. In the first half of 1991, just after consumer prices were freed, profits in the Czech food processing industry more than doubled, while farmers lost money. In one extreme Russian case the worker–owners of a milk plant paid themselves 45,000 roubles ($45) a month and the dairy farmers who supplied them only 2,500 roubles a month.

Only where a critical mass of competition exists, as in Polish meat-processing, can farmers command decent prices – in Poland, which has few trade barriers, these have reached world levels. Where falling domestic demand leaves a surplus, it cannot easily be exported: both the obvious markets – the EC and America – have been reluctant to lower trade barriers. Cheap as it may be, East European produce cannot compete on world markets with dumped western food. With such examples to follow, Eastern Europe's enthusiasm for free-market farming has begun to fade. Plans that look disturbingly like the EC's infamous common agricultural policy are cropping up in a number of countries. Even Hungary, which is a member of the free-trading Cairns group of agricultural exporters, established an Agricultural Marketing Regime in February, which allows guaranteed prices, production quotas and trade restrictions. Such 'temporary' market-rigging policies have a nasty habit of becoming permanent blots on the landscape.

Questions

1. According to the article, farming accounts for 20% of output in Eastern Europe. Find out the share of agriculture in GDP in other countries (this information can be found in *Eurostatistics* or in various OECD publications) and comment on your results.

2. Why do you think that private ownership of land might lead to higher prices? Can you think of any disadvantages of private ownership of land?

3. The article compares the small size of privatized farms with the large size of state-owned farms. What economies of scale do you think exist in farming? Are there diseconomies of scale in this industry?

4. What are the main features of the Common Agriculture Policy of the European Union? How does this policy affect Eastern European farmers?

PART H: PEOPLE AND METHODS

The Future is Not What It Used to Be

How accurate are economic forecasts? How could they be improved?

WHILE Albert Einstein is queuing to enter heaven, he meets three men. He asks about their IQs. The first replies 190. 'Wonderful,' exclaims Einstein. 'We can discuss my theory of relativity'. The second answers 150. 'Good,' says Einstein. 'I look forward to discussing the prospects for world peace'. The third mumbles 50. Einstein pauses. 'So what is your forecast for GDP growth next year?'

This old joke sums up most people's view of economic forecasters. Their reputation has been severely dented of late, not least because they failed to predict the strength of the world economic boom in the late 1980s and then, worse still, failed to warn of the consequent recession.

Are forecasts becoming less accurate? Financial deregulation and globalisation have made it harder to track the economy, so you might expect the answer to be yes. The facts, however, suggest otherwise.

The first table judges the forecasting record of Britain's Treasury over the past 13 years. It shows the mean absolute error (ie, adding up the differences between forecast and outturn each year

and ignoring whether it is plus or minus) of forecasts made each March for growth, inflation and the current account in the year ahead. During 1985-91 the average error for growth was 0.7 of a percentage point, compared with 1.2 points in the previous six years. The Treasury's forecasts of inflation and the current account also seem to have improved.

But such tests depend upon the time horizon. Looking at the forecasts which the Treasury made in the previous November of each year, its GDP forecasts for the period since 1985 seem to be more off beam than before, though it has got better at predicting inflation.

Victor Zarnowitz, an economist at the University of Chicago, has studied a large number of American forecasts over the past 30 years[1]. Taking the mean absolute error of predictions made at the end of each year for the year ahead, he finds that the accuracy of growth forecasts has hardly changed (see lower table). Inflation forecasts have become less accurate since the 1960s – but that is not surprising, given the surge in inflation in the 1970s.

Mr Zarnowitz also compared the average error of

these forecasts with the error from forecasts using a crude extrapolation of four-year moving averages of output and inflation. Professional forecasters will be relieved to know that the extrapolations proved much less accurate.

Further evidence that American forecasters have improved their aim comes from Blue Chip, an American newsletter, which polls about 50 economists each month. The mean absolute error of October forecasters for GDP growth in the following year fell from 1.1 percentage points in 1977-83 to 0.9 of a point in 1984-91.

Forecasters may be no worse than they used to be, but that is still not good enough. In particular, their biggest blunders tend to be at turning-points, when the economy dips into recession – the very time when forecasts are most needed.

Conventional forecasting relies upon a computer model built from the economist's favourite theory about how the economy works. Using past data, he tries to get the best fit for hundreds of equations that attempt to explain the relationships between economic variables. Assumptions about such things as tax rates, which cannot be forecast because they are decided by governments, are then plugged in and the computer cranks out an economic forecast.

Disappointment with the results of such models has encouraged some economists to test different kinds of crystal balls. Two developments pursued in America over the past decade have attracted growing interest. The first is vector auto-regressive models (VARs). These are much simpler, with far fewer variables than standard macroeconomic models. The process makes virtually no use of economic theory to establish causal links. Each variable is 'explained' largely by detecting patterns in its own statistical history; to make a prediction, the forecaster extrapolates this history into the future. Experience in America suggests that VAR models may be helpful in predicting turning-points.

A second development is the use of financial-spread variables (eg, the gap between short- and long-term interest rates) and business -confidence surveys as lead-ing indicators of activity. Past experience suggests that financial indicators are also good at spotting turning-points. For example, if short-term interest rates rise relative to long-term rates, this typically heralds an economic slowdown.

More recently, several British economists have gone down the same road. Gavyn Davies, an economist at the London branch of Goldman Sachs, has attempted to incorporate both of these techniques into forecasts for the British economy. Almost all standard economic models completely missed Britain's latest recession. But, claims Mr Davies, his new model, which uses both VAR and financial-spread indicators, would have given at least 12 months' warning of recession, if it had been available. It would also have predicted each of the previous two recessions and would have given no false alarms of recession during the past two decades.

Only time will tell whether VAR methods will continue to beat standard models. Their weakness is that they work only for as long as statistical relationships hold true, and in the past such models have often broken down almost as soon as they were used. In fact, this is just an extreme case of a general difficulty with all models based on past experience: they cannot cope with structural changes in the economy. Unprecedentedly high levels of debt in America and Britain, for instance, may have weakened the benefits of lower interest rates, which may explain why recovery has taken longer to happen than most economists predicted.

It is probably best to see VAR models and financial indicators not as alternatives to macroeconomic models, but as complementary, above all in helping to spot turning-points. Economic forecasting will never be 100% accurate, except by luck. But armed with every tool available, an economic forecaster just might earn his keep.

1 'Has Macro-Forecasting Failed?' Victor Zarnowitz, NBER working paper no. 3867.

British economic forecasts

Treasury forecasts[1] made in:	Mean absolute error of forecasts, percentage points	
	1979–84	1985–91
March		
GDP	1.2	0.7
Inflation	1.4	1.2
Current account	1.0	0.9
November		
GDP	0.5	1.4
Inflationp	2.7	1.4
Current account+	1.0	1.2

[1]for year ahead + as per cent of GDP

Sources: SG Warburg: updated by *The Economist*

American economic forecasts

	Mean absolute error of forecasts[1], percentage points		
	1959–67	1962–76	1969–89
GDP	1.2	1.2	1.1
Inflation	0.6	1.0	1.1

[1]Selection of private and government forecasts

Sources: Zarnowitz

Questions

1. Explain what is meant by a 'turning-point'. Suggest two ways in which these can be predicted.

2. Summarize the way in which economists forecast the future.

3. How accurate are such forecasts for the United Kingdom?

4. Do you think that it is methodologically valid to use past events to predict the future?

Ratonomics
Rat economics

Most people's idea of an economist is somebody slaving over a hot computer, torturing his data until he finds an equation which fits. That image may still fit most of today's economists, but not all. Some spend their time watching rats. A study by three American economists published in this month's *Economic Journal*, the bible of Britain's Royal Economic Society, seems to have taken John Maynard Keynes's concept of animal spirits (entrepreneurial zeal) rather literally. To test how individuals choose between two uncertain outcomes (eg, just as investors choose between financial instruments with different degrees of risk), the authors have used rats instead of people.

Most such experiments using humans are criticised because they are based on hypothetical outcomes or choices which involve tiny rewards. Using animals, claim the authors, is a cheap way to study choices between real, highly valued alternatives. The rats had to choose between two levers, repeatedly over several days. Each lever had different possible pay-offs (the number of cups of water it delivered) with fixed probabilities for delivering certain amounts of water to the thirsty rats. By offering the rats different choices in a series of experiments, the authors tried to test the shape of their 'indifference curve' – economists'

jargon for the range of different combinations of 'goods' (in this case risk and expected return) with which individuals are equally happy. To test the authors' pet theory (their own phrase), the rats were subjected to a 'two-tailed *t* test', a standard statistical tool for measuring the soundness of experimental results. This confirmed that their indifference curves, like their tails, were not linear but convex. Rats, it seems, would make risk-averse investors.

If rats are so good at making choices, perhaps they should be given a shot at economic forecasting. Given the record of most forecasters, rats may be a cheaper way to do that, too.

Questions

1. Explain what is meant by 'indifference curves' and draw an indifference curve diagram to illustrate the position in the text.

2. What methods of analysis are usually used by economists?

3. Why do you think so few economists use experiments?

In Praise of Hayek

The century's greatest champion of economic liberalism died on March 24th, at the age of 92

LIKE Maynard Keynes, Friedrich von Hayek achieved fame less for what he wrote than for what others said he wrote. The economic philosophy he developed over six decades, and especially during the 20 years he spent at the London School of Economics after 1931, was not, as so many now suppose, 'neo-conservatism'. Still less was it the underlying rationale for Thatcherism or Reaganomics, whatever those might be. And as it happens, the supposed 'godfather of monetarism' had no time whatever for the assumptions on which that narrow, technocratic doctrine is based.

None of these labels fits the great man. Call him instead an original thinker in the tradition of classical liberalism – perhaps the century's finest. Much of Hayek's work is difficult; all of it is idiosyncratic. His writings seem especially peculiar to economists trained in the modern Anglo-American way, because Hayek rejected that school's paradigm: the idea of a static system in which certain stable properties (many buyers, many sellers, perfect information, homogeneous goods) yield certain stable results (an optimal allocation of resources).

Hayek was interested in markets and economies as systems in flux. In his scheme, sequences of events, not states of affairs, were the object of study. Anglo-American economics starts by abstracting from change and time – and is then obliged to reintroduce them, with difficulty, to make its analysis more informative. Hayek, and others of the so-called Austrian school, put change and time at the centre from the outset.

Other themes seem to follow naturally from that perspective. They recur in almost everything Hayek wrote. The most crucial is the notion of a market as a process of discovery. Modern economies are vastly complicated. Somehow they must process immense quantities of information – concerning the tastes and incomes of consumers, the outputs and costs of producers, future products and methods of production, and the myriad interdependences of all of the above. The task of gathering this information, let alone making sense of it, is beyond any designing intelligence. But it is not beyond the market, which yields 'spontaneous order' out of chaos. Hayek looked on the miracle of the invisible hand with the same delight as Adam Smith. He celebrated it anew, and made it his mission to understand it.

A related idea from his early writings reappeared, after a pause, with new clarity in his later works – and especially in his last book, 'The Fatal Conceit', published in 1988. Hayek was always at pains to emphasise that civilisation did not come about by design: rather, it is human actions, with consequences both intended and (more often) unintended, that yield another sort of spontaneous order. Systems of human interaction are in competition with each other. Some thrive; others fail. With time, and many a reversal, history chooses the winners.

Hayek brought these ideas – the market as a processor of information, natural selection as a filter for systems of interaction – together in his critique of socialism. Like Smith, he took a kinder view of human nature than other writers in the liberal tradition. He asserted that, within small groups, co-operation is the instinctive mode of human interaction. Such groups depend on altruism and loyalty to survive; at that level, those traits are successful. But as the range of interaction extends, this sort of co-operation is no longer feasible. The socialist fallacy – the 'fatal conceit' – is to try to stretch small-group virtues such as loyalty and selflessness too far. Co-operation makes impossible demands on the ability of large groups to gather and process information; competition is the only way to regulate interaction on this scale. The attempt to extend co-operation beyond its natural limits is not just doomed to fail, it is also extremely dangerous. Competition requires no designer; co-operation on the large scale does. Socialism, the most ambitious and misguided form of large-scale co-operation, cannot be implemented without a strong central authority.

Hence another Hayekian theme: economic and political freedom are tied together. Hayek carried his distrust of the state to an implausible extreme. He argued, in effect, that governments could never legitimately pursue goals of their own – not even on behalf of 'society' (a term he disliked). Goals and values are for individuals themselves to choose. The state ought not to be a policy-maker with an agenda, but an arrangement of rules that allow people to go about their business in peace. Hayek was especially worried about the appearance of legitimacy that majoritarian democracy lends to the interventionist state. Where, he asked, is the minority's defence against the power of the majority?

Hayek's view, most of the economic powers that modern governments take for granted – from industrial policy to redistribution of income – are not merely ill-advised but immoral. Few could find that position satisfactory. The modern state may presume too much – but to deal with some economic ills, collective action (and hence the coercion that Hayek detested) is almost universally agreed upon. In some cases, moreover, it is simply inescapable.

Hayek's greatest weakness was that he had almost nothing to say about market-failure. This justification for state action is often falsely invoked – but sometimes the argument is convincing. In cleaning up the environment, for instance, the state must indeed intervene on behalf of society: externalities mean that free markets are unable to discover the outcomes that individuals seek.

If there is one label that Hayek would have accepted with pride, it is this: scourge of socialism. For decades his tireless attacks on what he saw from the beginning to be a profoundly evil system won him little praise from fellow economists. In the 1960s and 1970s he was a hate-figure for the left, derided by many as wicked, loony, or both. How marvellous it is that he lived to see communism collapse, as he said it would, with all its corruption, insanity and injustice laid bare.

Questions

1. Summarize Hayek's arguments.

2. How do his ideas differ from (a) 'the modern Anglo–American way' (that is, neo-classical economics), and (b) socialist ideas?

3. What criticisms could you make of Hayek's ideas?

The Search for Keynes

Was he a Keynesian?

Policies purporting to be Keynesian are in fashion once more. How many of these the great man would recognise, let alone endorse, is open to doubt.

IN MODERN economic debate, the term 'Keynesian' conveys two main ideas, usually muddled up together. One is that active fiscal policy (higher public spending, lower taxes) is a good remedy for recession. The other is that individual initiative and free enterprise have their limits; in this vaguest sense of 'Keynesian', the term has come to mean little more than 'that which is not conservative'. In the 1980s, governments in much of the industrial world, but especially in Britain and America, derided these notions. Now Bill Clinton, out of conviction, and John Major, out of lack of conviction, are embracing them anew.

What would Maynard Keynes make of the endurance of 'Keynesian' economics? He would be delighted, though not surprised (he was an immodest man), that nearly half a century after his death his name is still being shouted to and fro – in television studios, as well as in the economics departments of universities. But he might also be amused to see how the sides in these arguments line up. Keynes's complicated and often contradictory views have been reduced to simplicities that are often mere leftist prejudices.

Keynes was not of the left, and was contemptuous of unexamined prejudice (in others). Looking down, he might be unsure whether to applaud his followers or laugh at them. Placing Keynes in today's political spectrum would be difficult even if his views had been broadly constant: in any given work, his ideas are such an odd and original mixture that they refuse to fit familiar categories. What makes matters worse, though, is that his views were always changing. Nobody who has read much Keynes can avoid quoting him, because he was such a wonderful writer – but, thanks to his shifting opinions, there is no need ever to resist the temptation. Whatever your view on almost any topic in political economy, somewhere in Keynes is a sentence that puts it better than you could (and, admittedly, another somewhere else that refutes it).

Are you for free trade? Keynes was. To argue that trade barriers reduce unemployment, he said, 'involves the protectionist fallacy in its grossest and crudest form'. Elsewhere he wrote, with his usual finality, 'I believe in free trade because, in the long run and in general, it is the only policy which is technically sound and intellectually right.' Or do you favour protection – as did Keynes? 'I sympathise... with those who would minimise rather than with those who would maximise economic entanglement between nations. Ideas, art, hospitality, travel – these are the things which should of their nature be international. But let goods be homespun whenever it is reasonably or conveniently possible; and, above all, let finance be primarily national.'

Robert Skidelsky, in the newly published second volume of his excellent biography of Keynes, ponders these contradictions[1], and asks where Keynes's political sympathies lay. Keynes was certainly an elitist, Mr Skidelsky says. And he liked this aspect of the Conservative Party; Keynes thought it was splendid that, as he put it, 'the inner ring of the party can almost dictate the details and technique of policy.' That was just as it should be. But he wanted clever elitism, with men nearly as able as himself in charge. That is where the Tory party let him down; he felt that it not merely tolerated stupidity, but thought it a virtue. Keynes therefore directed much of his political and economic writing to the Labour Party – expressing his views in suitably friendly language. This may explain some of the inconsistencies.

In matters of economic theory, Keynes was scarcely any clearer. His most famous work, 'The General Theory of Employment, Interest and Money', published in 1936, is a difficult and confusing book. Keynes deliberately misrepresented the views of his opponents, crudely lumping their ideas together and calling them, mockingly, 'classical' (ie, obsolete). That angered many of his peers – few of whom were the purblind scholastics of popular mythology.

The resulting recriminations made clear-headed debate about the new theories nearly impossible. And since Keynes expounded the new ideas partly by contrasting them with a caricature of orthodox thinking (ie, with a theory that nobody actually believed), it made it harder to be sure what the new ideas were. Keynes, you might say, therefore got what he deserved. His own theories were almost immediately reduced to a variety of competing caricatures. And avowed disciples, not critics, undertook this task.

The need to distil from the 'General Theory' something that could be taught to one's students – few of whom could be expected to read or understand the great book itself – was paramount, especially for American academics. So, from the late 1940s, economists such as Paul Samuelson began to

spread the Keynesian gospel in the form of an income–expenditure diagram.

The big question in macroeconomics is whether and how long high unemployment might persist in an economy. Whatever else Keynes believed, he undoubtedly believed that high unemployment can linger indefinitely if left untreated. And the income–expenditure diagram can indeed portray such an 'equilibrium'.

For generations of undergraduates, and for more than a few finance ministers, here was all the macroeconomics you would ever need: the 'consumption function', public spending and the multiplier. A Keynesian revolution indeed. The problem of unemployment solved – and so easily. Nothing about prices (assumed to be fixed) or inflation. Nothing about the labour market. Nothing about interest rates, credit or the money supply. Nothing about the effect of changes in fiscal policy on public borrowing, on private wealth, or on anything else. Nothing about exchange rates, foreign investors or trade. Truly, Keynes was a genius.

The trouble is, the income–expenditure diagram does not examine or elucidate the claim that Keynes was at pains to make – namely, that high unemployment can be an equilibrium phenomenon. It just asserts it, sweeping the quarrel between Keynes and the 'classics' - ie, the bulk of the 'General Theory' – aside.

Much worse, the diagram implanted a dangerous prejudice firmly in the minds of countless economics students down the years. If economics is to help anybody make sense of the world, its first task must be to convey the extraordinary ability of the price system (ie, the market economy) to regulate itself in a variety of ways.

Much the most important thing in economics is the miracle of the invisible hand, whatever its failings, and however much it may need to be assisted by government intervention. Punk-Keynesian theory imbued many students with a brainless contempt for markets. Unemployment does not correct itself, they noticed: let's all be socialists. The economists that Keynes derided in the 'General Theory' had ideas about the market processes that ought to deal with unemployment. For instance, unemployment reduces wages, thereby stimulating the demand for workers. Or an excess of saving (ie, too little consumption) will cause interest rates to fall, thereby stimulating investment. A large part of Keynes's mission was to explain why these 'classical' mechanisms might fail to work - and why the slump of the 1930s might therefore fail to go away, unless the government itself took direct steps to cut unemployment and spur demand.

Thought of in this way, however, the 'General Theory' begins to seem rather less general. It looks more like a special theory – a theory of depressions. According to this view, Keynes was saying: market mechanisms, which plainly do assert themselves as a rule, can fail under certain circumstances, or fail to work quickly enough. A truly general model would place such ideas within a framework that let market forces play their part, with some theory to explain when and why 'Keynesian' factors might gain the upper hand.

Today all of his followers seem clear, at least, that Keynes believed in activist fiscal policy as a routine tool of economic management. Even this seems doubtful. Keynes certainly favoured a fiscal remedy for depressions – but that is not the same as advocating fiscal fine-tuning through the course of a normal business cycle. A theme that recurs in his work is a preference (echoing Hayek, please note, whose work he praised) for rules over discretion in economic policy; this sits uncomfortably with the 'kick-start' approach to economic management that modern Keynesians espouse.

In wartime memos Keynes argued against attempts to introduce 'Keynesian' budget policies. And, by modern standards, he was always extremely conservative on inflation, railing against its evils as passionately as any monetarist. The idea, popular now in Britain, that a bit of inflation is just the thing for an economy in recession finds no support in his work.

It cannot be to Keynes's credit, or to that of economics, that 56 years after the publication of the 'General Theory' there is still no consensus on 'what he really meant'. If economics is to be any sort of science, it can do without layers of hidden meaning; testable hypotheses are more the thing. It would be possible to push this criticism further, arguing that Keynes, for all his extraordinary skills as a writer–bureaucrat, made less of a contribution to economic science than he is generally credited with. You might even argue that Keynes's very obscurity was a chief reason why his name became an ism. He gained the public's attention as an essayist and commentator; claimed to be offering a theory for which, in the 1930s, there was plainly a need; but provided, in the event, a vessel for others to fill with their own ideas. That would be going too far.

For sheer originality of thought, Keynes was indeed one of the greatest economists of the century – perhaps even the greatest. But his achievement was not, as he claimed, that he refuted price theory and other classical conceits, replacing them with an equally coherent view of how economies work. Keynes's 'General Theory' was not, in fact, a general theory. And much modern macroeconomic research, in trying to explain persistent unemployment and other 'Keynesian' phenomena, is again using price theory in a way that the 'classics' would recognise. Keynes's achievement, rather, was to inspire a change in the character of economics. By force of intellect and personality, he altered its priorities – and thus its methods. The questions he sought to answer were about economics in the large: aggregate consumption, aggregate employment, aggregate investment and so on. This way of thinking, though hardly new, did not come naturally to those schooled in traditional price theory, where the task is to understand, say, the demand for one good rather than another, not the demand for all goods in the economy. By making such great claims for his own ever-changing ideas, and by ridiculing the straw man of classical orthodoxy to such devastating effect, Keynes moved the economics of aggregates – macroeconomics – to centre-stage. For decades, there it remained. It was a mixed blessing – but, undeniably, a remarkable achievement.

[1]'John Maynard Keynes: The Economist as Saviour, 1920–1937'. Macmillan

---

Questions

1. Draw and explain the income–expenditure diagram. What criticisms does the author make of this diagram?

2. What arguments does the article give against the Keynesian approach to unemployment?

3. What is the distinction between microeconomics and macroeconomics? Is the distinction clear?

What counterarguments would Keynesians give?

Data in the Raw

Prices and wages

% change at an annual rate

	Prices	Wages
Britain	2.4	3.8
Denmark	2.0	3.1
France	1.6	2.3
Germany	2.8	1.9
Holland	2.8	1.0
Japan	0.2	–0.2
Spain	4.4	5.2
Sweden	2.4	4.1
USA	2.6	2.9

Source: The Economist, 26 November 1994

Questions

1. What would you expect the relationship to be between changes in wages and changes in prices?

2. Examine the data in the above table (using either graphical or statistical methods) to see if there is a link between the variables.

3. Do you think that changes in prices leads to changes in wages, that the relationship is the other way round, or that there is no relationship? What data would you need to answer the question?

4. Why do you think the figures and relationships are different in different countries (for example, why prices rise faster in one country, wages in another)?

Data in the Raw

Inflation and unemployment

	Unemployment % rate
Britain	8.9
Denmark	11.7
France	12.7
Germany	8.2
Holland	7.6
Japan	3.0
Spain	24.3
Sweden	7.4
USA	5.8

Source: The Economist, 26 November 1994

Questions

1. What factors might explain the variations in unemployment shown in the table?

2. What does the Phillips curve suggest is the relationship between inflation and unemployment?

3. Draw a Phillips type curve to show the relationship between inflation and unemployment (use the data from page 77 for inflation). Does your diagram suggest a relationship between these two variables? (Note that the original Phillips curve used time-series data – that is, data for the United Kingdom over many years. The approach used here uses cross-section data – that is, data for several countries at one point in time – and is, therefore not strictly a Phillips curve.)

4. Find out (for example from *Economic Trends*) data on inflation and unemployment in the United Kingdom for the last 10 to 20 years. Plot the relationship and comment on your results.

NOTES

NOTES

NOTES

NOTES

NOTES

NOTES

NOTES

NOTES